Palgrave Studies in Risk, Crime and Society

Risk is a major contemporary issue which has widespread implications for theory, policy, governance, public protection, professional practice and societal understandings of crime and criminal justice. The potential harm associated with risk can lead to uncertainty, fear and conflict as well as disproportionate, ineffective and ill-judged state responses to perceived risk and risky groups. Risk, Crime and Society is a series featuring monographs and edited collections which examine the notion of risk, the risky behaviour of individuals and groups, as well as state responses to risk and its consequences in contemporary society. The series will include critical examinations of the notion of risk and the problematic nature of state responses to perceived risk. While Risk, Crime and Society will consider the problems associated with 'mainstream' risky groups including sex offenders, terrorists and white collar criminals, it welcomes scholarly analysis which broadens our understanding of how risk is defined, interpreted and managed. Risk, Crime and Society examines risk in contemporary society through the multi-disciplinary perspectives of law, criminology and socio-legal studies and will feature work that is theoretical as well as empirical in nature.

More information about this series at
http://www.palgrave.com/gp/series/14593

Imran Awan • Keith Spiller
Andrew Whiting

# Terrorism in the Classroom

## Security, Surveillance and a Public Duty to Act

palgrave
macmillan

Imran Awan
Centre for Applied Criminology
Birmingham City University
Birmingham, UK

Keith Spiller
Birmingham City University
Birmingham, UK

Andrew Whiting
Birmingham City University
Birmingham, UK

Palgrave Studies in Risk, Crime and Society
ISBN 978-3-030-01709-5 ISBN 978-3-030-01710-1 (eBook)
https://doi.org/10.1007/978-3-030-01710-1

Library of Congress Control Number: 2018959221



This Palgrave Pivot imprint is published by the registered company Springer Nature Switzerland AG
The registered company address is: Gewerbestrasse 11, 6330 Cham, Switzerland

# Contents

CHAPTER 1

# Introduction

**Abstract** The threat of terrorism has seen the implementation and development of new counter-terrorism strategies across the globe. The events of September 11, 2001, heralded the starting point of the ongoing Global War on Terror, and despite almost two decades having passed since then, further attacks that have targeted Western nations in particular have seen the continued expansion of counter-terrorism legislation. In the UK a notable contemporary example of this expansion has been the Counter-Terrorism and Security Act (2015) that has seen various different aspects of the public sector having a statutory requirement placed upon them to pay 'due regard to the need to prevent people from being drawn into terrorism' (HM Government, Prevent duty guidance. Available at https://www.legislation.gov.uk/ukdsi/2015/9780111133309/pdfs/ukdsiod_9780111133309_en.pdf, 2015: 5). Passed into law in 2015, this duty has also become a core component of the government's latest iteration of the flagship CONTEST strategy. One such area affected by this statutory duty is UK education, and it is this coming together of counter-terrorism and education that is the focus of our book. In this introduction we sketch out the background and importance of these events, explain our motivations and objectives, and lay out the book's structure to explain what each chapter will achieve.

**Keywords** Terrorism • Education • Prevent • Surveillance • Security

 
I. Awan et al., *Terrorism in the Classroom*, Palgrave Studies in Risk, Crime and Society,
https://doi.org/10.1007/978-3-030-01710-1_1

Since the events of September 11, 2001, that heralded the beginning of the ongoing Global War on Terror, but despite the elapse of so much time, a series of attacks targeting Western nations in particular have seen the expansion of counter-terrorism legislation and practices rather than their scaling down. The UK has been no exception to this trend, and this has culminated in an unprecedented formal encroachment of counter-extremism into the public sector. The most recent and overarching development in this regard is the government's publication of the third incarnation of its counter-terrorism strategy CONTEST (HM Government 2018) (with the sobriquet of CONTEST 3).

The Counter-Terrorism Security Act (CTSA) that came into law in 2015 imposed a statutory legal duty (often referred to as the Prevent Duty) upon all public sector workers to be aware and mindful of the vulnerabilities towards extremism. The CTSA imposes this duty on local authorities, schools, colleges, higher education institutions, health bodies, prisons and probation, and the police. For this book, education is the focus, and within this context this means that primary and secondary school teachers, teaching assistants, nursery school staff, registered childminders, as well as further education (FE) tutors and university lecturers are required to pay 'due regard to the need to prevent people from being drawn into terrorism' (HM Government 2015: 5) and look out for signs of vulnerability/radicalisation in the young people they teach and potentially report those who are 'at risk'. The CTSA elaborates on this formal expansion of counter-terrorism into education, explaining that protecting pupils from radicalisation should be understood as part of educator's wider safeguarding responsibilities and that education providers are expected to have 'clear policies in place to safeguard students and build their resilience to radicalisation in schools, further and higher education institutions' (HM Government 2018: 36).

As three academics teaching and researching within a UK University, our initial motivations for this book came specifically in relation to the CTSA and our own unease around what was now being legally required of us in our role as educators. This is broadly echoed in education in the UK, where primary schools, secondary schools, and the higher education (HE) sector (or post-secondary education, which included universities, sixth form colleges, and vocational training) all must comply with the new policy. The manner in which counter-terrorism and education had come together under the CTSA and the further entrenchment of this trend under CONTEST 3 were unprecedented and raised immediate and serious questions as to why this was occurring, how it would be operationalised, its appropriateness, its effectiveness, and the potential for harmful consequences. It should be noted that the CTSA *does* explicitly state that 'a specified authority must have particular regard to the duty to ensure freedom of speech' (HM Government 2015: 21), and CONTEST recognises that 'encouraging free speech and open debate is one of our most powerful tools in promoting critical thinking and preventing terrorist and extremist narratives taking hold' (HM Government 2018: 37). However, as active researchers with expertise across the fields of security, terrorism, surveillance, hate crime, and Islamophobia, we had experience with some of the areas and issues that this new duty had given rise to and subsequently began to explore recent developments at the intersection of counter-terrorism, counter-extremism, and education.

With this in mind, the overarching objective of this book is to chart contemporary developments in UK counter-extremism within UK education, and we explicitly document the current legislation which underpins the CTSA and then seek to document how those working in education have responded to the Act. The substantive focus of the book therefore is within the UK context, with the notable exception of Chap. 6 (discussed later in the chapter), which takes a deliberately international outlook. Within this overarching objective we seek to achieve a number of separate aims. First, we aim to provide the reader with a knowledge of 'how we got here' and explain the controversy that has surrounded the Prevent agenda prior to and since its expansion into UK education sector. Second, we aim to situate the recent developments in the UK within a broader international context to better understand how educational initiatives to counter extremism, promote peace, and develop resilience have been carried out elsewhere. Third, we aim to provide a wide-ranging critique of this expansion into education that draws on theories of surveillance and theories of power as well as our own empirical research with university lecturers in the UK.

We set out to achieve these aims and objectives by first outlining the broader context and exploring the key terminology surrounding terrorism and its prevention before setting this within the context of education. In Chap. 2, we consider the controversy and contestation that surrounds the concepts of radicalisation and extremism and how ambiguity here as well as around notions of Britishness creates difficulties in how the government shapes counter-terrorism policy. Chapter 3 considers the counter-terrorism legislation that has come about in the UK since the events of September 11, 2001, notably charting the development of the different versions of the CONTEST strategy. It is in this chapter that we pay particular attention to Prevent and the arrival of the CTSA that has seen UK counter-terrorism formally encroach into UK education among other areas of the public sector. The next two chapters shift the focus towards a more theoretical analysis of the application of counter-extremism. Chapter 4 contemplates the actualisation of the Prevent Strategy and investigates the monitoring and surveillance techniques that are a feature of it as well as the theoretical approaches that have been used to examine these sorts of processes. In this endeavour, we elaborate upon important concepts that are recurrent throughout this book, including bureaucracy, technology, risk control, and responsibilisation. Chapter 5 places an explicit focus on power when considering the manner with which UK counter-terrorism has encroached into the public sector and explains how the Prevent Duty operates as an extension of a broader strategy of neoliberal governance that seeks to manage the population. By reflecting on productive discourses of radicalisation, vulnerability, and resilience, the chapter demonstrates how the expansion of UK counter-terrorism into education is premised on a foundational 'risk knowledge'. Chapter 6 takes the attention off the UK and Prevent exclusively and investigates the way in which education has been utilised internationally as a means to prevent or reduce different forms of violence. In this chapter we consider the attention paid to the vulnerability of young people to radicalisation as well as the value placed in education as a means of preventing or disrupting this process as well as building student resilience. The majority of the chapter, however, is spent exploring and discussing a range of international educational initiatives that span the fields of Countering Violent Extremism (CVE), peace education, and citizenship education. Chapter 7 is based on an empirical study conducted by the authors that examines university lecturers' perceptions of their new public duty to pay 'due regard to the need to prevent people from being drawn into terrorism' (HM Government 2015: 5). In the chapter we reveal the tensions and contradictions felt by those that have been co-opted within the Duty and explore the anxiety that exists around monitoring and reporting as well as the ways in which lecturers have sought to resist this mandate. In our concluding chapter, we draw together the previous chapters to chart the core themes and reflect upon the implications of extending counter-terrorism into education for practitioners, students, and society.

## References

HM Government. 2015. "Prevent duty guidance". Available at: https://www.legislation.gov.uk/ukdsi/2015/9780111133309/pdfs/ukdsiod_9780111133309_en.pdf

HM Government. 2018. "Counter-terrorism strategy (CONTEST) 2018". Available at: https://www.gov.uk/government/publications/counter-terrorism-strategy-contest-2018

CHAPTER 2

# Contesting Terms: Radicalisation and Extremism

**Abstract** The challenge of extremism in recent decades to Western democracies and the resurgence of 'extremist' and 'radical' movements have led to growing concerns among academics, the public, and politicians (Eatwell and Goodwin, The new extremism in 21st century Britain. Routledge, London, 2010). While some, like Hussain (The Islamist. Penguin, London, 2007: 278), describe extremist rhetoric as the 'preamble to terrorism', for others the precise nature and extent of any association between concepts such as 'extremism', 'violent extremism', and 'radicalisation' remain less clear (Davies, Educating against extremism. Trentham Books, Stoke on Trent, 2008). The UK government has sought to define such terms (HM Government, Prevent Strategy. Available at: http://www.homeoffice.gov.uk/publications/counter-terrorism/prevent/prevent-strategy/prevent-strategy-review?view=Binary, 2011). However, a major problem with such terms is that they are value-laden. They are meaningful, and those meanings shift over time and place. Definitions shape how people interact in particular contexts, particularly at the levels of the personal, the group, and the social, and how they are dealt with (Hadley, J Soc Philos 40(3): 363–378, 2009; Hopkins and Kahani-Hopkins, Br J Soc Psychol 48: 99–113, 2009). Pantazis and Pemberton (Br J Criminol 49(5): 646–666, 2009) suggest, for example, that official political discourses and legislative measures in the context of the post-9/11 'war on terror' have led to the construction of the UK's Muslims as the 'suspect community'. This chapter will focus on definitions around



I. Awan et al., *Terrorism in the Classroom*, Palgrave Studies in Risk, Crime and Society,
https://doi.org/10.1007/978-3-030-01710-1_2

extremism and radicalisation and argue that the ambiguity of meanings and associations creates difficulties in how government shapes counter-terrorism policy. In particular, the wider empirical evidence we have gathered will be used in order to discuss the complexities surrounding these concepts and terms. Other extreme ideologies can also be identified, including animal rights extremism and anti-capitalist extremism. Each form of activism labelled 'extremism' is unique: it involves different individuals, groups, beliefs, motivations, values, and aspirations. Beyond this, extremism speaks to questions of 'community cohesion'.

**Keywords** Extremism • Radicalisation • Education • Terrorism • British Values

## Introduction

This chapter focuses on definitions that have emerged around extremism and radicalisation and argues that the ambiguity of meanings and associations creates difficulties in how public sector workers are meant to enforce their new public duty in safeguarding against extremist threats (see Chap. 7). As well as extremism being used as the justification to tackle threats within the public sector, other extreme ideologies appear to be given less importance because they cannot be easily identified, including animal rights extremism and anti-capitalist extremism. Each form of activism labelled 'extremism' is unique: it involves different individuals, groups, beliefs, motivations, values, and aspirations. Beyond this, extremism speaks to questions of 'community cohesion'. This chapter aims to examine how these concepts of extremism and radicalisation have informed counter-terrorism strategies within an educational context. Counter-terrorism policies and practices have now meant that all public sector workers, including doctors and teachers, must comply with statutory legislation that puts the onus upon them to combat extremism, including within the classroom (CTSA).

In order for us to have a better understanding of the counter-extremism framework, this chapter provides an analysis of two key terms within this field: extremism and radicalisation. We argue that the ambiguity around these terms means that the policy and legislation that have subsequently emerged (such as the CTSA) lack clarity and legal precision with detrimental consequences to civil society and UK education specifically. For Western democracies in recent decades, the challenge of understanding extremism and the resurgence of 'extremist' and 'radical' movements have led to growing concerns among academics, the public, and politicians (Eatwell and Goodwin 2010). This is mainly because being able to identify who is and who is not an extremist can lead to innocent people being arrested based on racial profiling and discrimination (Davies 2008). Indeed, the problem is not that these terms have not been defined at all; rather, it is the fact that they are open to interpretation and abuse. For example, ambiguity surrounding the definition of extremism has led to confusion around the requirement of violence herein and has seen the concept merged with distinctly non-violent action.

The UK government has sought to define such terms (HM Government 2011), but problems remain given their essentially contested and value-laden nature. Despite these problems, the definitions remain important when considering policies that emerge from them and their ability to shape how people interact in particular contexts, particularly at the levels of the personal, the group, and the social, and how they are dealt with (Hadley 2009; Hopkins and Kahani-Hopkins 2009). For example, Pantazis and Pemberton (2009) suggest that official political discourses and legislative measures in the context of the post-9/11 'war on terror' have led to the construction of the UK's Muslims as the 'new suspect community'.

Extremism arises not only from outside an identity grouping; it is also created by those inside as a way of marking out difference and belonging. A range of extremist organisations is described as including, but not overly concentrating on, Islamist extremism, both far-right and far-left. Lessons that should be learned from the conflict in Northern Ireland are compared to the approaches used presently to combat extremism, radicalisation, and terrorism. The manner in which counter-terrorism has developed is dynamic, and communities and those within the public sector may struggle to identify the threats they are supposed to manage within a terrorism context. This may also cause governments to drift into mass surveillance and other counter-productive counter-terrorism strategies (see Chaps. 3 and 4). In essence, government agencies, the police, and security services need to find the balance between the need to 'prevent people carrying out acts of political violence' and the threat to peoples' civil liberties (Wakefield and Fleming 2009: 77).

## Extremism and British Values in Education

The UK government has defined extremism as the 'vocal or active opposition to *fundamental British values*, including democracy, the rule of law, individual liberty and mutual respect and tolerance of different faiths and beliefs. We also include in our definition of extremism calls for the death of members of our armed forces, whether in this country or overseas' (HM Government 2011: 107, emphasis added). Extremism therefore can include multiple dimensions, with hate groups achieving their goals in different ways, that is by promoting ideology, promoting hatred of other racial or religious groups, exerting control over others, and targeting opponents (Awan and Blakemore 2013), for example, those that may question the requirement to 'tackle' extremism in all its forms or the inherent pejorative of being 'extreme' (linked to aforementioned comment). Despite these developments around extremism, there are many questions regarding the best way to prevent and disrupt extremism (Awan 2012), and ultimately a multiagency and community co-production may be needed to tackle threats around terrorism successfully. The UK government restructured its Prevent Strategy in 2011, and later through the CTSA 2015, it aimed to coordinate local and international responses to extremist crimes through coordinated strategies and proactive public state responses (see Chaps. 5 and 6). In the UK, there also needs to be a mechanism by which the terms extremism and radicalisation can be better understood and not subjected through a broad lens, which makes it problematic to understand and therefore difficult to enforce for frontline practitioners.

The ambiguity around the term extremism is dangerous, because it can lead to people being profiled based on their faith and religion, which may lead to further resentment and anger amongst particular groups within society. Hadley (2009: 367) states that '[i]t is not an exaggeration to say that there are as many definitions of terrorism in the literature as there are terrorist attacks in the real world. All of the leading definitions of terrorism, moreover, it is widely acknowledged, have their strengths and weaknesses and are more or less vulnerable to objection by counter-example…'.

There is no single pathway towards extremism, violence, and acts of terrorism; instead, there are a range of factors that lead to such incidents.

Extremism has become a nebulous term, with many different interpretations and definitions of what the term constitutes (Eatwell and Goodwin 2010). In the UK, tackling this threat from extremism has led to a wave of counter-terrorism policies and anti-terrorism legislation (see Chap. 3) (Terrorism Act 2006, Counter-Terrorism Act 2008, and the CTSA 2015). The term extremism is far too broad and being conflated with problematic associations with words linked to religion and faith such as 'fundamentalism', 'radicalisation', 'jihad', 'Islamism', and 'terrorism' (Davies 2008). Moreover, Eatwell (2006) argues that the term 'cumulative extremism' should be adopted as a means to define extremist threats to UK national security.

However, extremism as a concept has by implication the potential to marginalise and stigmatise a specific community, or as we argue, academic staff and public sector workers have been co-opted to become counter-terrorism practitioners. The Prevent Strategy does not help shed light on the meaning of extremism alongside British Values, but instead provides further problematic issues of interpretation and analysis. In defining extremism, Prevent has to focus on challenging and understanding the causes of what makes someone follow an 'extremist' or a 'radical' way of life and begin a process of engagement and support for those whom the government deems at risk of becoming extremists.

Within the education profession, contextualising and understanding what British Values constitute has become critical following recent terrorist attacks and the 'Trojan Horse' affair which impacted several schools across Birmingham. 'Trojan Horse' began with an anonymised letter that claimed hard-line 'Islamists' were plotting and planning to take over a number of schools in Birmingham. Amongst the allegations were that some of the schools had been promoting gender segregation and that children were not safeguarded against the risks of extremism. As the tribunal hearings against all the teachers have now found no wrongdoing, this chapter suggests that the debate about British Values and defining it as being part of an extremism narrative has impacted upon the wider education system. Chapter 7 will further demonstrate through qualitative research how the term extremism in this context has resulted in a polarised debate about religious conservatism and the actual threat of violent extremism within education.

## Who Is an Extremist?

As noted earlier, the label extremism for some groups and individuals can become a symbolic feature of their organisation, giving it credence and an opportunity to gather support and voice their opposition or concerns (Chakraborti and Garland 2009). The UK government does recognise that similar extremist ideologies are also considered a threat to UK national security from the violent gang culture depicted in the London riots in 2011, animal rights extremism, anti-abortionists, and anti-capitalist extremism (Eatwell 2006; Home Office 2011). As discussed earlier, there is no single pathway towards extremism; instead, there are a wide range of reasons why someone would hold such views depending on their beliefs, vision, motivations, aims, and values. These factors are based on a number of socio-economic, socio-demographic, and cultural factors which are linked to issues of identity and self-critique (Davies 2008). Although there are many different forms of extremism, counter-terrorism policies in the UK have not made any significant distinctions between different types of acts of terrorism or indeed extremism, and as such extremism could be applied to animal rights groups who have used tactics of fear and violence to promote an ideological cause they believe in (Home Office 2004).

Hadley (2009: 363) in his article 'Animal Rights Extremism and the Terrorism Question' raises serious questions and issues as regards whether acts of violence from animal rights protestors should be equated with acts of terrorism or extremism. He stated that '[p]erhaps animal rights extremists do not warrant the pejorative label "terrorists" but instead deserve to be known as freedom fighters consistently applying philosophically respectable views'.

Social movements and groups within animal rights organisations such as the Animal Liberation Front argue that their core purpose and moral rationale is to cause disruption of research into animal testing (Hadley 2009). However, the problem with such groups and movements is the strong links that can be made with forms of extremism, and as such, the goals they aim to achieve can often be undermined by the manner in which they protest, and as such, those acts can take away the credence of these movements. Hadley (2009: 364) states that '[a] strong association of animal rights with terrorism in the public consciousness could undermine the credibility of the animal rights movement and set the cause of animal protection back decades'.

Animal rights protest groups have been criticised for the nature of the acts of violence used in their demonstrations. These problems can be manifested in arguments made by such groups about the merits, morality, and ethics of scientific research, and therefore, violence is justified, as the use of violence for their actions may not be legal but they deem it to be proportionate and fair. Another major issue when labelling particular groups with the word extremist is the lack of a universal definition of what such terms mean. As noted earlier, Prevent aims to promote integration, cohesion, and community safety but has, critics argue, failed to tackle the wider issue of far-right extremism and instead paved the way for anti-Islamist groups such as Britain First.

The ambiguity around terms such as extremism means that Prevent and the CTSA 2015 have the potential of marginalising a single community and exacerbating a tone for groups such as Britain First, rhetoric that Islamism is on the rise in the UK and should be combated (Chakraborti and Garland 2009; Spalek 2010). The Prevent Strategy (HM Government 2011: 15) states that 'people involved in extreme right-wing terrorism have not received the same training, guidance or support as many of those who have engaged with Al Qa'ida or Al Qa'ida-influenced organisations'. Another reason the UK government argues that far-right extremism is a lesser threat than an Islamist one is because the literature available on far-right extremist groups is not as developed in a coherent policy framework. The Prevent Strategy (HM Government 2011: 20) argues that 'given the small number of relevant cases (and the absence here of extreme right-wing terrorist organisations and formal groups) our understanding of how people become involved in extreme right-wing terrorism is inevitably less developed than it is for terrorism associated with Al Qa'ida'. However, following the rise in referrals from people with a far-right background shows that the trend may be changing (Spalek and Lambert 2008).

The review into Prevent also found that a majority (80%) of respondents in the consultation believed that Prevent should address the wider problems of far-right extremism (HM Government 2011). Whilst the UK government has recognised the threat posed by Islamist terrorist groups and as such banned certain Islamist groups which promote violence, similar far-right groups like Britain First remain operational (the main difference between these groups being the ideologies and motives). This process requires a deeper understanding of socio-economic, racial, ethnic, and cultural barriers that exist today between law enforcement agencies and communities who lack trust in the legal, criminal, and political systems.

This may be also because communities and now public sector workers perceive themselves as being treated unfairly (Spiller et al. 2017; Hickman et al. 2011). The long-term effects of such tactics upon staff and students may also lead to them becoming disaffected and isolated as shown by Spalek et al. (2008), who found that police accountability and transparency over their actions was a problem and a reason for tensions between police and community engagement. As a result, academic staff, due to poor training and understanding of key terms, may be labelling only certain students as extremists.

## Britishness and Education

Miah (2015: 31) argues that the debate around Britishness demonstrates the political nature of education which is influenced by questions around integration and assimilation (see Chap. 7). He argues that the current discourse around Britishness provides a non-negotiable association with British Values which is enshrined in principles that must show a demonstration of loyalty and citizenship. The Trojan Horse affair has also led to a new debate regarding the role of British Values. The former Prime Minister David Cameron (2011) stated that these values should be about the rule of law and freedom of religion. These values are now enshrined within the school education documentation. For example, the Department for Work and Education (2014) states schools must promote British Values. The government goes a step further and has stated all schools have a duty to actively promote these fundamental British Values. Cantle Report (2001) states that the values in a school system allow for a greater sense of citizenship, cohesion, and integration. Despite these attempts to create a greater sense of cohesion, the introduction of British Values has in fact created more confusion within the higher education sector regarding free speech, extremism, and radicalisation. But what are British Values?

The Prevent public duty states that all public sector institutions must have a due regard for supporting and challenging extremist behaviour. Without much more guidance, the UK's leading University and College Union attests that the duty seriously threatens academic freedom and freedom of speech (Spiller et al. 2017). Interestingly, the legislation designed to promote British Values is actually impeding open debate, because the new duty specifically requires universities to fill out a risk assessment form in advance, which flags up speakers whom they view as being extremist, radicals, and 'risky', and therefore, rather than challenging assumptions or stereotypes, are instigating a conservative approach to risky subjects (Spiller et al. 2017). This risk assessment undermines due process rights, undercutting the right to liberty and to freedom of speech.

Furthermore, the problem with such definitions is that they will shift over time, and similarly the term British Values and extremism will also evolve and change. Indeed, Hillyard (1993) argued that Irish communities in the 1960s were being labelled as extremists and had therefore become a 'suspect' community following the conflict in Northern Ireland. Similarly, Pantazis and Pemberton (2009) have also argued that the post-9/11 political discourse on extremism and the 'war on terror' rhetoric has led to British Muslims becoming the 'new suspect' community. Furthermore, these definitions can be considered as value-laden and subjective and, as a result, can be problematic when it comes to trying to understand the behaviour and patterns of individuals, groups, and movements described as extremists (Sunstein 2009; Hopkins and Kahani-Hopkins 2009). In 2006, this unprecedented threat from extremism was described by the former British Prime Minister Tony Blair at the time as:

> the poisonous propaganda of those people that warps and perverts the minds of younger people. it's a very long and deep struggle, but we have to stand up and be counted for what we believe in and take the fight to these people who want to entice young people into something wicked and violent but utterly futile. (Cited in the Guardian 2006)

The ambiguity surrounding the terminology of these key concepts can also lead to difficulties in contextualising and understanding what those in the public sector must do to enforce the government mandate. Central in this effort is the Channel Duty Guidance document (HM Government 2015) that aims to protect vulnerable people from being drawn into terrorism. Herein lies a list of 22 vulnerability identifiers that are there to serve as the 'vulnerability assessment framework' to aid public sector workers when deciding whether to make a referral to the authorities about an individual's potential to be drawn into terrorist and extremist violence. The risk factors are as follows:

**Engagement**

1. Grievance/injustice
2. Threat

3. Identity, meaning, and belonging
4. Status
5. Excitement, comradeship, or adventure
6. Dominance and control
7. Susceptibility to indoctrination
8. Political/moral motivation
9. Opportunistic involvement
10. Family and/or friends support extremist offending
11. Transitional periods
12. Group influence and control
13. Mental health

**Intent factors**

14. Over-identification with a group, cause, or ideology
15. Them and us thinking
16. Dehumanisation of the enemy
17. Attitudes that justify offending
18. Harmful means to an end
19. Harmful objectives

**Capability factors**

20. Individual knowledge, skills, and competencies
21. Access to networks, funding, or equipment for terrorism
22. Criminal capability

These 22 factors (sometimes referred to as the ERG22+) provide an exceptionally broad remit for those who can be considered risky or vulnerable. Such breadth poses important questions as to the consistency and universality with which these factors are being applied as too does the ambiguity of the language included here. With such breadth and subjectivity being written into this list of factors, the guidance does provide the caveat that these are only factors that should not be used in isolation. Yet each of the terms and phrases remains difficult to define. A further problem that arises is that the definition of extremism (discussed earlier) specifically cites those individuals as being more extreme, because they do not fulfil the 'British Values' framework.

Whilst media coverage and debate about extremism has focused on negative stereotypes and links with people regarded as terrorists, critics argue that many individuals once regarded as extremists are now considered high-profile political activists and reformers (Davies 2008). Furthermore, in particular, the word extremism has in the past been used to describe people such as Mahatma Gandhi, Nelson Mandela, Malcolm X, and Dr. Martin Luther King, who are now accepted as being pioneers for change and individuals who have made an important contribution towards social activism and social community cohesion. As Hopkins and Kahani-Hopkins (2009: 101) state, 'Dr King sought to re-define the meaning of extremism and moderation so as to re-shape the terms of reference with which his activism was to be judged. Specifically, his contrast between these forms of extremism (love and hate) left no place for moderation or passivity: all right-thinking people must identify with the project of mass activism'.

Thus, this pervading debate as to who is and who is not an extremist is rooted in the political versus legal interpretation of extremism and terrorism (Githens-Mazer and Lambert 2010). The analogy that 'one man's terrorist is another man's freedom fighter' provides us with the example of the problems when it comes to defining extremism and indeed terrorism. Despite the conceptual challenges involved in attempting to define the word extremism, there is little doubt that some people labelled as extremists have had the capacity to inflict harm and damage upon society in the pursuit of their ideological causes. Thus the problem for international governments is the need to balance civil liberties whilst also preserving security (Bleich 2010). Grayling (2009), for example, argues that the major problem for democracies across the world is the terrorist threat and also how values and liberalisation are protected within communities.

## Rethinking Radicalisation and Education

Just as extremism and terrorism are problematic to define, the term radicalisation has also caused tension (Pantazis and Pemberton 2009). There is no universal definition of radicalisation, yet a number of pathways exist. The current terminology around radicalisation is too broad and could include a process of violent behaviour in the pursuit of changing a political situation through violent aims and objectives. Radicalisation has been defined by the UK government as 'the process by which a person comes to support terrorism and forms of extremism leading to terrorism' (HM Government 2011: 108). The term radicalisation therefore should cover processes by which individual's behaviours, beliefs, attitudes, and activities change over time. This change in behaviour requires an analysis and construction of the theoretical models that examine the causes and reasons why and how someone becomes radicalised.

One such theory is the 'conveyor belt model' which views radicalisation as a process that involves progression from radical interpretations of faith to actual terrorist acts of violence. The theory is often used by US think tanks to assess the radicalisation process; however, it lacks critical detail and, in particular, has little robust evidential background with regard to preventing radicalisation. Another pathway to radicalisation is where individuals are searching for an identity. This forms the social identity theory which is based upon an assertion that radicalisation develops as a result of, first, people being confused about their identities, and second, individuals searching for a meaning of their role within society or in a community. Tajfel and Billig (1974) argue that this sense of social isolation leads to a perception of discrimination and prejudice, which, in turn, leads to individual's reactions being shaped from a belief that violence is a legitimate justification for what is deemed as 'oppressive' foreign policies, counter-terrorism laws, and Islamophobia (Hillyard 1993).

For Tufyal (2007), however, this is based more on societal characteristics that view radicalisation through individual's intimate interactions with extremists who often influence these individuals into committing acts of terror. He argues that the radicalisation process starts with a perception of inequality within society, which is often based on a lack of trust with UK politics, security, and law enforcement agencies (Tufyal 2007). He states that 'the intensity of such feelings is reinforced by experiences of discrimination and racism, a sense of blocked social mobility; and a lack of confidence in the British political system' (Tufyal 2007: 6).

Other theoretical studies of the process of radicalisation include the 'situational activity theory' which views radicalisation as a social movement and social progression (Campbell and Connelly 2008). This model uses societal causal factors to describe how people are influenced by actors that use different modes of recruitment tactics such as personal meetings, social activism, and indoctrination (Wiktorowicz 2005). This form of radicalisation may occur in prisons through gang membership, which can provide moral status, acquiescence, and privilege.

Most of these theories, however, are used by policy makers to inform law enforcement agencies and practitioners as to what might lead to radicalisation; however, they are subjective in nature and in turn fail to identify the actual 'root' causes that lead to someone being vulnerable to radicalisation. It is clear that socio-economic and cultural factors do play a role in determining who becomes radicalised (Silke 2005). Therefore, one of the important points of radicalisation within an educational setting is the process of transition from naive and vulnerable individuals to would-be terrorists. For example, Sageman (2008) in his book *Leaderless Jihad* argues that radicalisation occurs in the online world where people are able to engage in online chat rooms and forums, which are ideal places for people to join terrorist groups and become radicalised in a virtual world of social movements.

Whilst theoretical underpinnings around radicalisation assume a set of factors, there is also a problem in defining the 'pre-criminal space', that is, people being radicalised by so-called non-violent means. Clearly, this can lead to difficulties for those who work in the public sector. There is a problem in relation to what the pre-criminal space actually means and the secrecy surrounding the Channel intervention programmes. For example, in 2015, a postgraduate student named Mohammed Omar Farooq was reported by his university to the Prevent Channel intervention process because he was reading a terrorism book. It could be argued the university was only following the guidance. As a result, such broad and ambiguous guidance is less than clear for those tasked with performing this new-found role. The indicators, as outlined earlier, lack precision, and secondary information is often required—for instance, knowing a student's family are 'extremist'. More significant perhaps is that the evidence base that informs the guidance is less than obvious. The university in question apologised for, in its words, 'a misjudged situation', but for Farooq the impact has had a frightening experience and has left him emotionally drained after he had been questioned for simply reading an academic textbook.

## Conclusion

In the context of education, radicalisation must be looked through a broader spectrum of issues such as deprivation, foreign policy, and self-identity issues, and a lack of integration and feelings of grievances do impact upon the way people turn to terrorism both within and outside of a prison setting (Silk 2005). As noted earlier, there are many different interpretations of the word extremism, radicalisation, and British Values. It does appear that the new public duty imposed upon public sector workers is rooted in ambiguous language that is likely to cause anger, alienation, and ultimately abuse of power (Fanshawe and Sriskandarajah 2010). Extremism remains vague and at best lacks clarity, leading to a perception that government policy is being shaped on a subjective process which may, in effect, marginalise the public sector workers (Lambert 2011). Davies (2008) argues that the term extremism should cover a wide range of factors and should not be simply viewed as being confined to Islamist extremism. This perception that extremism equates to violence is confused political will with acts of terrorism. As Hopkins and Kahani-Hopkins (2009: 99) state that 'Dr King was an extremist outsider and they called for those attracted to his project to revert to using the courts to redress the wrongs of segregation. In depicting Dr King in this way, the clergymen were drawing on a long history of thought that celebrates the virtues of moderation'.

This sense of moderation and understanding is primarily based upon how individuals regarded as extremists have different viewpoints and interpretations of causes they believe to be legitimate. This exploration of opinions cannot always be measured, but they are important social indicators of patterns of behaviour. Hopkins and Kahani-Hopkins (2009: 100) argue that '[e]xtremists are often depicted as people who see the world in simplistic black-and-white terms rather than more nuanced shades of grey. This perspective is well illustrated in work linking extremism to individual deficiencies in cognitive complexity'.

Many of these theories which relate to extremism have made associations and links with Muslim groups and what is perceived as religious extremism (Loza 2007; Schmidt et al. 2005). Indeed, one of the major reasons why people or groups deemed to be considered extremists hold such views is the notion that these individuals feel a sense of alienation, isolation, and despair (Prus 2005). One of the core reasons of this isolation is what some groups or individuals deem as unpopular counter-terrorism policing, anti-terror legislation, foreign policies, and political values. This can also have a detrimental effect upon communities regarded as extremists; for example, Briggs et al. (2006: 46) argue that:

> [a] lazy parlance in which the words "extremist" and "radical" have become interchangeable has meant that any Muslim expressing anything other than unremitting support for the government is under suspicion. Not only does this close down the space for important debates about issues which are causing understandable frustration, but it also means that government tends to speak only to those deemed "moderate" voices or the usual suspects.

Indeed, for public sector workers, the problem of interpretation is likely to cause further difficulties when trying to identify vulnerabilities and safeguarding against extremist threats. The definitions of both extremism and radicalisation remain too broad and could have the potential of making students be treated as suspects. Rethinking counter-extremism policy is vital if we are to challenge hate and tackle terrorism in the future. It must, however, start with a protection of liberty, freedom of speech, freedom of expression, and freedom of thought and movement without fear that people will be viewed as being too extreme and radical. We also argue that the ambiguity in the language of such terms is likely to lead to cases such as Mohammed Farooq and others who have been unfairly targeted because they have been deemed to be an extremist.

## References


Awan, I. 2012. "'I'm a Muslim not an Extremist:' How the Prevent Strategy has constructed a 'Suspect' Community", *Politics & Policy*, 40 (6): 1158–1185.

Awan, I and Blakemore, B. 2013. *Extremism, Counter-Terrorism and Policing.* London: Ashgate Publishing.

Briggs, R., Fieschi, C., and Lownsbrough, H. 2006. *Bringing it home: Community-based approaches to counter-terrorism.* London: Demos.

Bleich, E. 2010. "Faith and State. British policy responses to 'Islamist' extremism". In *The New Extremism in 21st Century Britain,* edited by R. Eatwell and M.J. Goodwin. London: Routledge: 68–84.

Cameron, D. 2011. "PM's Speech at Munich Conference". Number 10 Downing Street. Available at: http://www.number10.gov.uk/news/speeches-and-transcripts/2011/02/pms-speechatmunich-security-conference-60293

Campbell, C. and Connolly, I. 2008. "A Model for the "War Against Terrorism"? Military Intervention in Northern Ireland and the 1970 Falls Curfew", *Journal of Law and Society*, 33 (3): 341–375.

Cantle Report. 2001. *Community Cohesion: A Report of the Independent Review Team.* London: Home Office.

Chakraborti, N. and Garland, J. 2009. *Hate Crime: Impact, Causes and Responses.* London: Sage Publications.

Davies, L. 2008. *Educating Against Extremism.* Stoke on Trent: Trentham Books.

Department for Work and Education. 2014. "Guidance on Promoting British Values in Schools". Available at: https://www.gov.uk/government/news/guidanceonpromotingbritish-values-in-schools-published

Eatwell, R. 2006. "Community Cohesion and Cumulative Extremism in Contemporary Britain", *The Political Quarterly*, 77(2): 204–216.

Eatwell, R. and Goodwin, M.J. (eds.) 2010. *The New Extremism in 21st Century Britain.* London: Routledge.

Fanshawe, S. and Sriskandarajah, D. 2010. *You Can't Put Me in a Box: Super-Diversity and the End of Identity Politics in Britain.* London: Institute for Public Policy Research.

Githens-Mazer and Lambert, R. 2010. "Islamophobia and Anti Muslim Hate Crimes: a London case study", *European Muslim Research Centre.* Available at: http://centres.exeter.ac.uk/emrc/publications/IAMHC_revised_11Feb11.pdf

Grayling, A.C. 2009. *Liberty in the Age of Terror: A Defence of Civil Liberties and Enlightenment Values.* London: Bloomsbury.

Hadley, J. 2009. "Animal Rights and the Terrorism Question", *Journal of Social Philosophy*, 40 (3): 363–378.

Hickman, J., Thomas, L., Silvestri, S., Nickels, H., 2011. "Suspect Communities: Counter-terrorism policy, the press and the impact on Irish and Muslim communities in Britain". Available at: http://www.statewatch.org/news/2011/jul/uk-london-met-suspect-communities-findings.pdf

Hillyard, P. 1993. *Suspect Community: People's Experiences of the Prevention of Terrorism Acts in Britain.* London: Pluto Press.

Home Office. 2004. *Animal Welfare and Human Rights: Protecting People from Animal Rights Extremists.* London: Home Office Communications Directorate.

Home Office. 2011. "Proscribed terror groups or organisations". Available at: http://www.homeoffice.gov.uk/publications/counter-terrorism/proscribed-terror-groups

HM Government. 2011. *Prevent Strategy.* Available at: http://www.homeoffice.gov.uk/publications/counter-terrorism/prevent/prevent-strategy/prevent-strategy-review?view=Binary

HM Government. 2015. "Prevent Duty Guidance: For Higher Education Institutions in England and Wales". Available at: https://www.gov.uk/government/uploads/system/uploads/attachment_data/file/445916/Prevent_Duty_Guidance_For_Higher_Education__England__Wales_.pdf

Hopkins, N. and Kahani-Hopkins, V. 2009. "Reconceptualizing 'extremism' and 'moderation': From categories of analysis to categories of practiced in the construction of collective identity", *British Journal of Social Psychology, 48*: 99–113.

Hussain, E. 2007. *The Islamist.* London: Penguin.

Lambert, R. 2011. "Neo Conservative Ideology Trumps Academic Research and Practitioner experience Responding to Prevent 2011". *Muslim Council of Britain.* Available at: http://www.mcb.org.uk/comm_details.php?heading_id=121&com_id=2

Loza, W. 2007. "The Psychology of Extremism and Terrorism: A Middle-Eastern perspective", *Aggression and Violent Behaviour*, 12: 141–155.

Miah, S. 2015. *Muslims, Schooling and the Question of Self-Segregation.* UK: Palgrave Macmillan.

Pantazis, C. and Pemberton, S. 2009. "From the 'Old' to the 'New' Suspect Community: Examining the Impacts of Recent UK Counter-Terrorist legislation", *British Journal of Criminology*, 49(5): 646–666.

Prus, R. 2005. "Terrorism, tyranny, and religious extremism as collective activity: Beyond the deviant, psychological and power mystiques", *American Sociologist*, 36: 47–74.

Sageman, M. 2008. *Leaderless jihad: Terror networks in the twenty first century*. Philadelphia, PA: University of Pennsylvania Press.

Schmidt, C., Joffe´, G., & Davar, E. 2005. "The Psychology of Political Extremism", *Cambridge Review of International Affairs*, 18: 151–172.

Silke, A. 2005. "Fire of Iolaus", in Bjorg, T. (ed.) *The Root Causes of Terrorism: Myths, reality and ways forward*, New York: Routledge: 242–248.

Spalek, B. 2010. "Community Policing, Trust, and Muslim Communities in Relation to New Terrorism", *Politics & Policy*, 38(4): 789–815.

Spalek, B. and Lambert, R. 2008. "Muslim Communities, Counter-Terrorism and De-Radicalisation: A Reflective Approach to Engagement", *International Journal of Law, Crime and Justice*. 36(4): 257–270.

Spalek, B., El Awa, S. and McDonald, L. 2008. "Police-Muslim Engagement and Partnerships for the Purposes of Counter-Terrorism: An Examination", *Arts and Humanities Research Council*. Available at: http://www.religionandsociety.org.uk/uploads/docs/2009_11/1258555474_Spalek_Summary_Report_2008.pdf

Spiller, K., Awan, I., and Whiting, A. 2017. "'What does terrorism look like?': University lecturers' interpretations of their Prevent duties and tackling extremism in UK Universities, Critical Studies on Terrorism". Available at: http://www.tandfonline.com/doi/full/10.1080/17539153.2017.1396954

Sunstein, C. 2009. *Going to Extremes: How Like Minds Unite and Divide*. Oxford: Oxford University Press.

Tajfel, H. and Billig, M. 1974. "Familiarity and categorization in intergroup behaviour", *Journal of Experimental Social Psychology*, 10: 159–170.

The Guardian. 2006. "Blair backs MI5 terror warning". Available at: http://www.guardian.co.uk/world/2006/nov/10/terrorism.politics

Tufyal, C. 2007. "The Role of Muslim Identity Politics in Radicalisation (a study in progress) (April)", *Department for Communities and Local Government: London Communities and Local Government*. Available at: http://www.communities.gov.uk/documents/communities/pdf/452628.pdf

Wakefield, A. and Fleming, J. 2009. *The SAGE dictionary of policing*. London: Sage.

Wiktorowicz, Q. 2005. *Radical Islam Rising: Muslim Extremism in the West*. Maryland: Rowman and Littlefield.

CHAPTER 3

# The Development of UK Counter-Terrorism Policy and Legislation

**Abstract** The former prime minister of the UK, David Cameron, in 2010, spoke at a conference in Munich about security, radicalisation, and multiculturalism, sparking a controversial debate about how the UK monitors and deals with extremism. This chapter will examine counter-terrorism legislation that dates back to the response to 9/11. It will also explore the current UK Prevent Strategy 2011 and examine the role of the CTSA and new public sector duty (which will be discussed in further detail in a later chapter). In 2010, the UK government review of counter-terrorism legislation and policy included examining the broader counter-terrorism strategies, that is, CONTEST/CONTEST 2. The focus of CONTEST is to reduce the risk to the UK from international terrorism, and the CONTEST has four key strands, which include Prevent. The others are Pursue, which aims to stop terrorist attacks; Protect, which endeavours to strengthen systems against terrorist attacks; and Prepare, which aims at preparing against a terrorist attack by mitigating its impact. For the purposes of this chapter, we will be examining the Prevent strand of CONTEST whose origins lie contextually in post-9/11 and 7/7 when Muslims became a 'suspect' community. This chapter, however, will now also argue that wider counter-terrorism policies in the UK have led to an erosion of trust. Furthermore, such strategies are driven by state-led policies, embedded within vague and ambiguous local initiatives that lack both clarity and detail, and in effect, people act as informants and provide intelligence on each other and identify would-be



I. Awan et al., *Terrorism in the Classroom*, Palgrave Studies in Risk, Crime and Society,
https://doi.org/10.1007/978-3-030-01710-1_3

extremists and terrorists. This chapter will detail the emergence of counter-terrorism policies and provide a review of some case studies that have involved counter-terrorism legislation.

**Keywords** Counter-terrorism • Prevent • Extremism • Security: Muslims

## Introduction

Since the events of 9/11 in the United States, and several terrorist attacks in the UK such as the London bombings in 2005, Woolwich in 2013, and the Westminster attack in 2016, issues relating to terrorism, radicalisation, and extremism have been at the forefront of recent public debate. Indeed, following the Iraq War, home-grown terror attacks, and the upsurge of young people travelling to Syria, the UK has enacted a new wave of counter-terrorism strategies and policies, including the new UK Counter Terrorism and Security Act 2015 (HM Government 2015). In this chapter we demonstrate how new counter-terrorism policies such as this are likely to amplify the impact upon civil society and, in particular, that of specific populations and newly co-opted roles. The chapter progresses by examining counter-terrorism legislation introduced as a response to 9/11, as well as the UK Prevent Strategy and the role of the CTSA in the public sector. However, before discussing the wider impact of counter-terrorism policies within education, this chapter seeks to provide a historical lens in terms of how counter-terrorism policies have emerged.

Ball and Webster (2003) argue that following the 9/11 attacks, a massive expansion of security-surveillance capacities around the globe ensued. There was also an accompanying set of legislative powers such as the 'Patriot Act' in the USA which ushered in systematic surveillance; this means the state has the powers to monitor phones, emails, and computer use in general. While technology can aid prevention and detection of extremist activity, there have been notable design flaws, and aspects such as privacy and human rights issues need to be addressed (see Chaps. 4, 5, and 7). The UK counter-terrorism strategy CONTEST has four key themes in tackling the threat from terrorism. They are to 'protect', 'pursue', 'prepare', and 'prevent' a terrorist attack. Whilst counter-terrorism legislation and policies have developed since the 9/11 terror attacks, recent developments through the CTSA 2015 have meant that all public sector workers have a legal duty to tackle any extremist behaviour (CONTEST 3).

In 2010, the UK government review of counter-terrorism legislation and policy included examining the broader counter-terrorism strategies, that is, CONTEST/CONTEST 2 and 3. The focus of CONTEST is to reduce the risk to the UK from international terrorism, and CONTEST has four key strands, which include Prevent. The others are Pursue, which aims to stop terrorist attacks; Protect, which endeavours to strengthen systems against terrorist attacks; and Prepare, which aims at preparing against a terrorist attack by mitigating its impact. CONTEST 3 has not really changed the focus of the UK government's counter-terrorism strategy, but the new refreshed strategy shifts the focus on the framework to counter terror threats. This starts with a process that includes a focus on domestic investigative capabilities. The new and revised strategy also weaves into counter-terrorism policies and practices the role of integration. Using the Prevent delivery model, it specifically highlights tackling the causes of extremism, providing early intervention, and using rehabilitation to tackle extremist behaviour (HM Government 2018).

This chapter will detail the emergence of counter-terrorism policies and provide a review of some case studies that have involved counter-terrorism legislation. It begins with a thematic analysis of the suspect community thesis based on counter-terrorism legislation and policies. Our key argument here is that the suspect community thesis (see Chap. 2) impacts on all types of communities within HE and those who are part of the new public duty to prevent extremism. In order for us to have a more contextualised understanding of the suspect community, we will first provide the historical basis for how Muslim communities were targeted by counter-terrorism policies before moving on to consider the manner in which counter-terrorism legislation has encroached into wider aspects of civil society.

## The Suspect Community Thesis

The notion of 'suspect' communities was first coined by Hillyard (1993) in his critique of how communities in Northern Ireland had fallen under this label. His analysis has a number of similarities in the context of how Muslim communities today could be viewed in a similar light. For example, profiling, hard-line policing, stop and search, surveillance, and detention have become policy-led strategies that attempt to deal with terrorism. Whether inadvertently or not, they have the potential to stigmatise the entire populations, such as Irish people living in the UK during the conflict in Northern Ireland, and now the Muslim community in the UK. Hillyard (1993) characterised the impact of counter-terrorism legislation such as the Prevention of Terrorism Acts (PTAs) upon the Irish community in Britain during the 1980s. His in-depth study included 115 interviews with participants and concluded that the PTAs had in effect 'constructed' a 'suspect' community from the 'Irish living in Britain, or the Irish people travelling between Ireland and Britain' (Hillyard 1993: 257–8). Hillyard contended that people were 'suspect' 'primarily because they [were] Irish' (Hillyard 1993: 7). He also suggested that this was a result of institutionalised, anti-Irish racism. Pantazis and Pemberton (2009) suggested a similar parallel between the reality faced by the Irish in the 1980s and that faced by Muslims in Britain today.

There has been a rise in Islamophobic hate incidents in the UK since the 9/11, 7/7, and Woolwich attacks, and this has led to claims that Muslim communities are unfairly being targeted by the police, far-right groups, the media, politicians, and counter-terrorism legislation and institutional Islamophobia. Indeed, the Association of Chief Police Officers (ACPO) has seen a rise in anti-Muslim hate incidents following the Woolwich attacks in the summer of 2013 (Feldman et al. 2013). This spike in anti-Muslim prejudice has further strengthened the narrative of official suspicion and has led to the current debate that Muslims are the 'new suspect community' (Awan 2012; Pantazis and Pemberton 2009; Ryan et al. 2009). These claims are magnified by statistics that indicate that over 75% of people arrested for terrorism charges since 2001 have been released without charge (Choudhury and Fenwick 2011). Indeed, counter-terrorism tactics and policing initiatives such as Project Champion in Birmingham (UK) have also highlighted why Muslim communities feel under suspicion. Project Champion involved the West Midlands' police use of covert and overt CCTV cameras across Birmingham, in predominately Muslim areas, paid for by a Terrorism Allied Fund (Awan 2012).

The overall conclusions drawn from an independent review conducted by Sarah Thornton from Thames Valley Police clearly point towards a lack of 'transparency' by the police and indicate that police actions damaged police-community relations in the suburbs of Birmingham where the cameras were installed. The Prevent Strategy has also come under the fiercest criticism for failing to engage in a positive manner with Muslim communities and for stigmatising them (Khan 2009; Yaqoob 2008; Awan 2012). For example, Choudhury and Fenwick (2011: 15) argue that '[i]n some areas, Preventing Violent Extremism (PVE) was thought to be undermined by the lack of transparency'. It is this lack of 'transparency' and mismanagement of public funds that led to the overall criticism of strategies such as Prevent.

Similarly, Awan (2012) argued, following the new Prevent Strategy 2011, that the label of the 'new suspect community' is reinforced by the manner in which the Prevent Strategy 2011 focuses upon Islamist extremism at its core. Furthermore, in the same way that the PTA facilitated the construction of the Irish as a suspect community, the implementation of legislation such as the Anti-Terrorism and Security Act 2001, the Prevention of Terrorism Act 2005, the Terrorism Act 2000, and the Terrorism Act 2006 has led to the creation of a new Muslim 'suspect' community (the legislation will be discussed in more detail later in the chapter).

Pantazis and Pemberton (2009: 649) define a 'suspect' community as a subgroup of the population that is singled out for state attention as being 'problematic'. Specifically in terms of policing, individuals may be targeted, not necessarily as a result of suspected wrongdoing, but simply because of their presumed membership to that subgroup. Race, ethnicity, religion, class, gender, language, accent, dress, political ideology, or any combination of these factors may serve to delineate the subgroup. Using this definition, they propose a pyramid structure that starts at the base with how media reporting of stories pertaining to Muslim communities may unfairly label them as 'Islamists', 'fundamentalists', and 'Jihadists', thus beginning the process of creating the 'suspect' community. At the top of the pyramid, counter-terrorism legislation and hard-line policing, such as house arrest, stop and search, law enforcement monitoring, and pre-charge detention, generate a more hostile arena led by law enforcement agencies and the state, which cements the categorisation of Muslim communities as 'suspects'. At the pyramid's pinnacle, 'applying to only a handful of individuals ... the legal evidence may be stronger but a criminal trial has been considered impossible due to the sensitive nature of the evidence' (Pantazis and Pemberton 2009: 649). Our definition for a new suspect academic community is based on the recent legislation that requires all public sector workers to report signs of extremism. We argue that the suspect community notion has moved away from a traditional community towards academic staff and others in the public sector. Our definition for a new suspect community consists of the following: using counter-terrorism legislation as a tool to impose all public sector workers (including academic staff in HE) to become the eyes and ears of the state. Failure to report potential signs of extremism or missing the signs of extremism can lead to a failure to comply with the legal duty to uphold the legislative framework.

A related problem with the strategy and the creation of a 'suspect' community has been the blurring of the strategy's main aims, which risks linking counter-terrorism with community cohesion and community development. Many of these community services are offered by local councils tasked with mainstreaming Prevent initiatives. The Prevent Strategy creates problems where the government shoehorns certain counterterrorism projects into a community-based approach that adopts community cohesion and builds community resilience as a means to tackling extremism. The convergence of community cohesion and community development programmes with preventing extremism risks blurring the boundaries between counter-terrorism and community cohesion. A more serious concern with Prevent involves the issue of local authorities and councils mapping certain projects for particular communities, since the mapping initiative appears to have targeted many Muslim communities across England and Wales (HM Government 2011).

Several extracts from the Prevent Strategy (HM Government 2011: 17–8, 31–2, 43–9) further reveal how the Muslim community could be deemed as the 'new suspect' community. First, it notes how the key driver for radicalisation remains a problem within the Muslim community: 'we believe that radicalisation—in this country—is being driven by an ideology that sets Muslim against non-Muslim'. Second, it raises concerns as regards theological ideas concerning Islam. In particular, the strategy notes that 'the Government designated Islamic studies as a strategically important and vulnerable subject', and further adds that '[t]he FCO and DCLG also sponsored a series of "road shows" by Muslim community groups around the country involving lectures, debates and cultural events aimed at promoting a mainstream message of Islam on a number of key issues, including terrorism'.

While these programmes' aims are for better community cohesion, they clearly target a certain faith (Islam) and a particular religious ethnic group (Muslims) as opposed to offering similar projects for a different religious or faith group. Third, Prevent discusses the problem for police officers whom the government recognises will undertake the task of promoting Prevent initiatives within Muslim communities. 'We understand concerns among some police officers that nothing should be said in the context of *Prevent* which inadvertently undermines community engagement and the work they do to encourage people to report suspicious activity and criminal behaviour' (HM Government 2011: 32). Fourth, it speculates about the profile of extremists, and in particular describes the issue of social exclusion within Muslim communities, noting that '[i]t has been argued in particular that some second or third generation Muslims in Europe, facing apparent or real discrimination and socio-economic disadvantage, can find in terrorism a "value system," community and an apparently just cause'. And last, it discusses the growing importance of gathering intelligence within local communities, and adds that '[w]hile Prevent must not be used as a means of systematically gathering intelligence on people or communities, it is essential that accurate and relevant information about the terrorist threat is shared by the police with local Prevent partners'.

Recent studies also reveal that counter-terrorism policies, such as Prevent, may actually have contributed to a spate of hate crimes committed against Muslims because of the manner in which Prevent has been used within Muslim communities and institutions. Githens-Mazer and Lambert's (2010) article on hate crimes found that a number of British mosques had been vandalised with graffiti and set ablaze because of the conflict within the UK concerning counter-terrorism policies and the increasing media association of words such as 'terrorism' and 'Jihad' with Islam and Muslims. The words jihad and terrorism have often been used in the same anecdote to describe Muslims as a 'problem group'. However, the association of both terms—in particular through media reporting—is dangerous, and therefore risks causing Islamophobic reactions against Muslim communities.

Research with different communities is essential to reach the kinds of understandings necessary to develop solutions to complex social problems and also to examine the impact of counter-terrorism legislation upon those within academic, communities, families, and individuals in a wider context. The implications of multiculturalism and the balance between civil liberties and security are two such issues, especially in post-9/11 and 7/7 Britain. At the same time, any sociological and criminological research must be able to fully engage those whose views and experiences are sought. Indeed, for criminologists the issue and impact of doing research which can benefit wider society is at the forefront of academic literature and discourse.

Innes et al. (2011) identified tensions between the Prevent and Pursue strands of CONTEST and emphasised the need to understand diversity within Muslim communities and identified that both young men and Muslim women aged 45 and above have lower levels of trust towards the police than corresponding non-Muslims. Overall, however, they found that Muslims have more confidence in the police than non-Muslims. In contrast to this, Choudhury and Fenwick's (2011) report on counter-terrorism impact upon Muslim communities has analysed the impact at a 'grassroots' level in Birmingham, Glasgow, London, and Leicester. In all cases, the arguments can be framed around a central idea of the 'suspect' community, both traditionally being used to target Muslims and now moving into the area of HE.

The 'symbiotic relationship' between terrorism and CONTEST has also been neglected, despite indications that counter-terrorism tends 'to escalate rather than alleviate levels of perceived threat, actual violence and alienation of the base population' (Breen-Smyth 2007: 265; Ranstorp 2009). As such, there is a need for a contemporary, cultural, and realist criminological perspective that examines systems of control and power relations, given that 'to explore cultural dynamics is to explore the dynamics of power – and to build the basis for a cultural critique of power as well' (Ferrell et al. 2008: 7). According to the Choudhury and Fenwick (2011) study, which examined Muslim communities' responses towards counter-terrorism policy and legislation, it was found that Muslim communities, organisations, and groups felt the terrorism legislation was both heavy-handed and disproportionate. The chapter will now provide a brief snapshot of counter-terrorism legislation and two empirical case studies that show the level of impact counter-terrorism legislation may have. Whilst these impacts historically have affected Muslim communities, we will later on discuss how recent events have now impacted upon the wider suspect community.

## UK Terrorism Legislation Post-9/11 and 7/7

Following the 9/11 and 7/7 attacks, the UK government has been in the process of enacting a number of counter-terrorism legislations all aimed to protecting national security. This includes the Anti-Terrorism, Crime and Security Act 2001, the Terrorism Act 2000, the Prevention of Terrorism Act 2005, the Terrorism Act 2006, and the Counter-Terrorism Act 2008. The problem with these legislations is that they have had the potential to stigmatise communities and risk alienating them as civil liberties are eroded (Gearty 2005). The Terrorism Act 2000, for example, created a number of controversial offences that appear to have had an impact upon Muslim communities. Whilst the police were given wider powers to stop and search under Section 44 of the Terrorism Act 2000 (which allows the police to stop and search anyone without the need for 'reasonable suspicion' provided the powers are authorised by a senior police officer and confirmed by the Home Secretary), they also were given powers to detain suspects after arrest for 14 days (this was then increased to 28 days under the Terrorism Act 2006, and is now 14 days). Moreover, the new provisions included offences that allowed the police to arrest individuals who were suspected of incitement towards a terrorist act, or people who were providing training for terrorist purposes and providing instructions in the use of firearms, explosives, and chemical and biological weapons.

In particular, Schedule 7 of the Terrorism Act 2000 has been tainted by allegations that it targets Muslim and Asian communities. For example, statistics show that between April 2011 and March 2012, almost 70,000 people were questioned by officers at British ports and airports and 45% of these detainees were of Asian or Asian British origin (Liberty 2012). Schedule 7 gives the police the power to stop and detain individual and search passengers both at ports and airports to try to determine whether they are terrorists or not. They can also be detained, as in the case of David Miranda (the partner of *The Guardian* journalist Glen Greenwald), for up to nine hours and their possessions can be examined. The problem with this, however, is the frequent assumption that someone is guilty of being a terrorist without actual evidence of criminality in the first instance.

For example, in a case brought before the European Court of Human Rights, by Sabure Malik, a British national, it was revealed that Schedule 7 can have a long-lasting effect on someone. After being detained under Schedule 7, following a trip to the Hajj (in Mecca, Saudi Arabia), he was marched through the terminal by police officers and bundled in the back of a police van. Malik would later describe the incident as a humiliating experience, and like Miranda, he had his possessions examined. In his case, the detective inspector noted that an officer under Schedule 7 'does not require any reasonable grounds to stop a person and conduct any such examination' (Cited online in the Malik Case Report 2013).

It is because of this intrusion of privacy and an absence of reasonable suspicion that a consultation took place between September and December of 2012 to examine the implications of Schedule 7 (Home Office 2013). It found that many respondents were concerned with its disproportionate use against Muslim communities. For example, questions such as 'Which Mosque do you attend?' or 'How often do you pray?' were viewed as negative and Islamophobic. The Anti-terrorism, Crime and Security Act 2001 was introduced after the September 11 attacks. It was intended to cut off terrorist funding and promote better partnership work between governmental departments. However, after the 7/7 attacks, the Prevention of Terrorism Act 2005 was enacted and replaced Part 4 powers under the Anti-terrorism, Crime and Security Act 2001, which led to the subsequent controversial control orders regime which could be used against suspected terrorists.

Control orders were limited and could only be imposed for a period of up to 12 months at a time (Fitzpatrick 2003). The restrictions included house arrest, who a person can speak to, who a person can meet with, or when a person can leave his home. If a control order was breached without reasonable excuse, it would result in a prison sentence (Brandon 2004). Control orders have now been abolished and replaced with Terrorism Prevention and Investigation Measures (T-Pims). T-Pims include the following: (1) a limitation of holding a suspect without charge (i.e., based on a premise of conducting a more thorough investigation followed by possible charge and conviction); (2) a suspect will be allowed to use a mobile phone and the Internet, subject to conditions allowing for a greater freedom of association; and finally (3) T-Pims will expire after 2 years unless new evidence emerges of involvement in terrorism.

Moreover, the shift of focus is now on evidence that is more robust where previously there was a requirement for the Home Secretary to show 'reasonable suspicion', and this has now changed to include the phrase 'reasonable belief'. Therefore, T-Pims will not forcibly remove suspects (objectionable to many minority communities who have felt that counter-terrorism legislation has marginalised and stigmatised them), meaning that suspects will now be required to stay at home overnight for up to 10 hours where previously it had been 16 hours. However, the impact of such reforms remains Kafkaesque because they in fact mean that suspects will continue to be electronically tagged, report regularly to the police, and could face exclusion from particular places as well as the prevention of travel overseas. Furthermore, the current system cannot escape the stigma attached to control orders and may well continue to have the potential of fostering alienation of the Muslim communities in Britain and potentially act as a recruitment tool for extremist groups (Githens-Mazer and Lambert 2010).

Indeed, the new wider threat from global terrorism meant the UK government brought in the Terrorism Act 2006, which also created a number of 'new' offences. These included the 'encouragement' and/or 'glorification' of terrorism; the dissemination of terrorist publications and the preparation of terrorist acts; and finally, training for terrorist purposes. The offence of 'direct encouragement' requires that a person who commits the offence of publication of a specific statement shows that there is a 'direct encouragement' of a terrorist act. This could mean that an individual could be reckless about the contents of their statement and still be prosecuted as a result.

Another problem is that these new powers potentially make us less safe and could result in driving dissent underground and alienating minorities. The problem with the current offence of 'glorification' is that it has a real potential of limiting 'freedom of expression'. This could mean people are prosecuted for speeches they deliver and the manner in which they publish such statements (Amnesty International Report 2007). As noted earlier, the offence of 'glorifying terrorism' could also have a detrimental effect upon people's freedom to express their opinions, making people concerned about the language they use and the manner in which they approach sensitive issues and topics, in case their words are construed as incitement to terrorism. For example, the case of Samina Malik, also known as the 'Lyrical Terrorist', shows how vague this statute can be. In her case, she was initially convicted for the poetry she wrote because it was deemed to be inciting acts of terrorism. On appeal, her conviction was quashed on the basis that a jury could not ascertain the links between her poetry and actual acts of terrorism (Glendinning 2008). The aforementioned legislation illustrates the duplicity of the legal system in the UK, arising because counter-terrorism legislation is geared towards preventing terrorism and not towards providing criminal justice remedies.

This gives rise to the 'terror of prevention' felt by whole communities (Hillyard 1993: 262; Pantazis and Pemberton 2009: 654). In itself, counter-terrorism legislation has always appeared in a piecemeal manner and is often reactive towards terrorist attacks. Whilst the earlier text discussed this from a historical perspective, the text that follows will focus on the new CTSA 2015 and the early impacts it may have upon HE and British Universities.

## British Universities and the CTSA 2015

The Prevent Strategy 2011 mandates universities have a role in combating extremism, radicalisation, and terrorism. The Home Secretary (at the time) Theresa May suggested that universities had become 'complacent' in tackling forms of radicalisation and extremism on their campuses.

> I think for too long there's been complacency around universities. I don't think they have been sufficiently willing to recognise what can be happening on their campuses and the radicalisation that can take place. I think there is more that universities can do. (Gardham 2011)

Government rhetoric that institutions should take a more leading role in preventing extremism has now been extended to education colleges, university societies, and student groups. In doing so, it risks making universities police their students in a much more difficult arena. The notion that academic staff and lecturers might possibly act as intelligence sources to gather and disseminate evidence concerning their students risks loss of teacher-student trust. It also falls into a wider definition of the new 'suspect academic' community. Although academic staff and lecturers should be there to promote learning, teaching, and research, it appears that the government's focus now on university complacency in dealing with extremists does risk making student (and teacher) experience at universities more tense and difficult.

Universities UK has examined the ways into preventing extremism and radicalisation on university campuses. In its report published in 2011, it concluded that the higher education sector needed to be more vigilant and aware of the challenges posed by extremism (Universities UK 2011). Furthermore, the Department for Business, Innovation and Skills identified 40 English universities that are at particular risk of extremism, radicalisation, and recruitment on campus (Slack 2011). The government has used this research, which reveals that more than 30% of people convicted for a terrorist offence in the UK have attended a university or a higher education establishment (Department for Business, Innovation, and Skills 2007). This is important since the research has been used as a template for government policy in making universities more accountable and dealing with potential extremists on campuses.

Similarly, Simcox et al. (2010) found that only one-third of terrorist offences committed were by people who had attended university. This new sharp focus upon universities is problematic in that it makes universities part of the overall Prevent Strategy 2011, and risks leading to state interferences and government-sponsored tactics of getting lecturers to look out for signs of extremism. In a time of austerity when universities are facing huge budget cuts, this in turn could lead to universities shouldering the role of the police in countering extremism, which again presages a loss of student trust in the role of HE and their lecturers.

The problem for universities in tackling extremism has already been clearly highlighted by a high-profile case that illustrates how universities could now be deemed to be part of the radicalisation process. While studying for a postgraduate qualification in counter-terrorism, Rizwaan Sabir downloaded an al-Qaeda training manual from the Internet. He was arrested under the Terrorism Act in May 2008 for downloading extremist material, but was released after seven days without charge (BBC News 2008). The case highlighted the dangers of tackling extremism on university campuses as students could now be prosecuted for downloading material from the Internet if a jury deemed it to be a material that could be used for a terrorist purpose. In 2011, Sabir was paid £20,000 in damages by the Nottinghamshire police following his arrest. He successfully won his case for false imprisonment and also Nottinghamshire police's conduct, which was deemed to be in breach of human rights legislation. The case also raised important issues concerning how the police and universities implement counter-terrorism policies (such as Prevent), and the profound impact that counter-terrorism arrests can have upon a person's family life. In Sabir's words:

> This is finally some vindication and we can say proudly that I have proved to many, many people who may have suspected that I was a terrorist that I am actually innocent and always have been ... It shows and it proves that [the police] were wrong to have behaved the way they did. They were wrong to put me through the torturous experience they did and they have finally accepted that. (Jones 2011)

Rizwaan Sabir also expressed concerns about how universities, in his view, have become less accountable on issues pertaining to counter-terrorism policies, and argued that universities should do more to build trust with their students. 'Because there is no public authority in the whole of the United Kingdom that can hold British universities to account, only a public inquiry can reveal the possible extent of malpractice' (Sabir 2011; see also Jones 2011). The shift in Prevent policy now means that universities should do more to ensure their students are not following a path of extremism. However, with this policy comes a stark warning that Islamic associations at universities and other faith associations, such as Christianity, Sikh, or Jewish group, will also have to play a stronger role in combating extremism. The Prevent Strategy 2011 will have a counter-productive effect as it will create an atmosphere among young British Muslims of isolation and anger that could lead to more people following a path of extremism (Awan 2012). At the moment, the Prevent Strategy 2011 does not provide any tangible or credible evidence as to how universities can tackle the threat of extremism on campuses; instead, it implies by its counter-terrorism narrative that academics will know who is and who is not an extremist.

The CTSA has sought to address this void, and a sharp focus has now been placed on universities that puts a legal statutory duty on all public sector workers to counter extremism. The Counter-Extremism Strategy places doctors, mental health practitioners, teachers, and lecturers as key people who can assist in helping tackle violent extremism. The act was 'fast-tracked' though Parliament (House of Lords 2015), and as Theresa May—then Home Secretary—stated:

> From 1 July the new statutory Prevent duty for specified authorities will commence... Once this has been fully implemented it will require local authorities, the police, prisons, probation services, schools, colleges – and yes, universities too – to have due regard to the need to prevent people from being drawn into terrorism... This will ensure that Prevent activity is consistent across the country and in all those bodies that work with those who may be vulnerable. (Home Office 2014)

The CTSA effectively asks those in positions of authority to monitor those they supervise. We know monitoring has a significant effect on the subject (Ball 2009), and this is well covered by disciplines such as Surveillance Studies (Lyon et al. 2012). For example, previous work has investigated the surveillance of school children (McCahill and Finn 2010), employees (Ball 2010), and offenders (Nellis 2006). Following the terror attacks in London and Manchester, there is a need for an urgent independent review of counter-terrorism measures and the effectiveness of strategies such as Prevent and the new public duty (see Chap. 7). The CTSA has been a source of contention between the government, ministers, the media, academia, and the public. On the one hand, it is being viewed as a vital aspect of the broader counter-terrorism strategy and something that is necessary to protect national security. On the other hand, critics argue it disproportionately impacts upon individual liberty and has a particularly stigmatising effect on those working within the public sector.

Media reports have served to highlight the misunderstanding that may pervade around the Prevention Strategy, examples of which include a student who was questioned by his university for reading a book entitled *Terrorism: A Reader* because it created suspicion despite the student claiming this was a recommended reading text, and speakers being banned on university campuses because they are deemed to be 'risky' speakers. Alongside these worrying accounts, however, is the concerning spate of recent terrorist attacks in Westminster, Manchester, and London Bridge. The role of counter-terrorism policies should be in preventing violent extremism, and the scope of its remit now means that all public sector workers must by law play security roles because it is deemed that they are best equipped to counter radicalisation.

## Conclusion

As this chapter has demonstrated, the reactionary methods of terrorism legislation have been poorly conceived. In fact, it has left considerable questions with regard to how best to approach terror threats and whether legislation can be an effective method if it infringes upon basic human rights and civil liberties. It also has emerged that new suspect communities have been formed in the way that now academic staff are being probed and positioned as terrorism practitioners. This is worrying as it is likely to create problems between academic staff and the student community. The historical nature of terrorism policies has always been focused on one or two types of communities. The new CTSA is likely to go a step further and actually criminalise those it deems are at the front line of tackling extremism.

## References

Amnesty International Report. 2007. "Human rights in United Kingdom of Great Britain and Northern Ireland". Available online at: www.amnesty.org/en/region/uk/report-2007

Awan, I. 2012. "The impact of policing British Muslims: a qualitative exploration", *Journal of Policing, Intelligence and Counter Terrorism*, 7(1): 22–35.

Ball, K. 2009. "Exposure: Exploring the Subject of Surveillance", *Information, Communication & Society*, 12(5): 639–657.

Ball, K. 2010. "Workplace Surveillance: An Overview", *Labor History*, 51(1): 87–106.

Ball, K. and Webster, F. (eds). 2003. *The Intensification of Surveillance: Crime, Warfare and Terrorism in the Information Age*. London: Pluto Press.

BBC News. 2008. "Student Was Studying Terrorism." *BBC News*. Available online at: http://news.bbc.co.uk/1/hi/england/nottinghamshire/7415685.stm

Brandon, B. 2004. "Terrorism, human rights and the rule of law: 120 years of the UK's legal response to terrorism", *Criminal Law Review*, December: 981–997.

Breen Smyth, M. 2007. "A Critical Research Agenda for the Study of Political Terror", *European Political Science*, 6(3): 260–267.

Choudhury, T. and Fenwick, H. 2011. *The Impact of Counter-Terrorism Measures on Muslim Communities*. Manchester: Durham University.

Department for Business, Innovation, and Skills. 2007. "Promoting Good Campus Relations, Fostering Shared Values and Preventing Violent Extremism in Universities and Higher Education Colleges." Department for Business, Innovation, and Skills. Available at: http://www.bis.gov.uk/assets/biscore/corporate/migratedD/ec_group/22-07-HE_on

Feldman, M., Littler, M., Dack, J., and Copsey, N. 2013. "Anti-Muslim Hate Crime and the Far Right", *Teeside University*. Available at: http://tellmamauk.org/wp-content/uploads/2013/07/antimuslim2.pdf

Ferrell, J., Hayward, K.J., and Young, J. 2008. *Cultural Criminology: An Invitation*. London: Sage.

Fitzpatrick, J. 2003. "Speaking law to power: the war against terrorism and human rights", *European Journal of International Law*, 14(2): 241–264.

Gardham, D. 2011. "Universities Complacent over Islamic Radicals, Theresa May Warns", *Daily Telegraph*. Available online at http://www.telegraph.co.uk/news/uknews/terrorism-inthe-uk/8558499

Gearty, C. 2005. "11 September 2001, counter-terrorism, and the Human Rights Act", *Journal of Law & Society*, 32(1): 18–33.

Githens-Mazer and Lambert, R. 2010. "Islamophobia and Anti Muslim Hate Crimes: a London case study", *European Muslim Research Centre*. Available at: http://centres.exeter.ac.uk/emrc/publications/IAMHC_revised_11Feb11.pdf

Glendinning, L. 2008. "'Lyrical terrorist' has conviction quashed'", *The Guardian*. Available at: http://www.theguardian.com/uk/2008/jun/17/uksecurity.ukcrime

Hillyard, P. 1993. *Suspect Community: People's Experiences of the Prevention of Terrorism Acts in Britain*. London: Pluto Press.

Home Office. 2013. "Review of the Operation of Schedule 7: A Public Consultation". Available online at: https://www.gov.uk/government/uploads/system/uploads/attachment_data/file/212548/WEB_-_2013_07_15_Review_of_the_operation_of_Schedule_7_A_Public_Consulta___.pdf

Home Office. 2014. "Home Secretary Theresa May on Counter-Terrorism." Available at: https://www.gov.uk/government/speeches/home-secretary-theresa-may-on-counterterrorism.

HM Government. 2011. *Prevent Strategy*. Available at: http://www.homeoffice.gov.uk/publications/counter-terrorism/prevent/prevent-strategy/prevent-strategy-review?view=Binary

HM Government. 2015. "Prevent Duty Guidance: For Higher Education Institutions in England and Wales." Available at: https://www.gov.uk/government/uploads/system/uploads/attachment_data/file/445916/Prevent_Duty_Guidance_For_Higher_Education__England__Wales_.pdf

HM Government. 2018. "Counter-terrorism strategy (CONTEST) 2018". Available at: https://www.gov.uk/government/publications/counter-terrorism-strategy-contest-2018

House of Lords/House of Commons Joint Committee on Human Rights. 2015. "Legislative Scrutiny: Counter-Terrorism and Security Bill – Fifth Report of Session 2014–2015". Available at: http://www.publications.parliament.uk/pa/jt201415/jtselect/jtrights/86/86.pdf

Innes, M., Martin, C. Roberts, Helen, I., Lowe, T. and Lakhani, S. 2011. "Assessing the Effects of Prevent Policing: A Report to the Association of Chief Police Officers". Available online at: http://orca.cf.ac.uk/23060

Jones, S. 2011. "Student in Al-Qaeda Raid Paid £20,000 by Police", *The Guardian*. Available online at http://www.guardian.co.uk/uk/2011/sep/14/police-pay-student-damages-al-qaida

Khan, K. 2009. "Preventing Violent Extremism (PVE) & PREVENT, A response from the Muslim Community", *An-Nisa Society*. Available at: http://www.an-nisa.org/downloads/PVE_&_Prevent_-__A_Muslim_response.pdf

Liberty. 2012. "Liberty's Response to the Home Office's Review of the Operation of Schedule 7". Available at: http://www.liberty-human-rights.org.uk/pdfs/policy12/liberty-s-response-to-the-consultation-on-the-operation-of-schedule-7-dec-20.pdf

Lyon, D., Haggerty, K. D., and Ball, K. 2012. "Introducing Surveillance Studies". In *Routledge Handbook of Surveillance Studies*, London: Routledge: 1–12.

Malik, S. 2013. "Malik v United Kingdom, Fourth Section Decision", *European Court of Human Rights*. Available at: http://hudoc.echr.coe.int/app/conversion/pdf/?library=ECHR&id=001-121698&filename=001-121698.pdf

McCahill, M., and R. Finn. 2010. "The Social Impact of Surveillance in Three UK Schools: "Angels", "Devils" and "Teen Mums"", *Surveillance and Society*, 7(3/4): 273–289.

Nellis, M. 2006. "Surveillance, Rehabilitation, and Electronic Monitoring: Getting the Issues Clear", *Criminology & Public Policy*, 5(1): 103–108.

Pantazis, C. and Pemberton, S. 2009. "From the 'Old' to the 'New' Suspect Community. Examining the Impacts of Recent UK Counter-Terrorist legislation", *British Journal of Criminology*, 49(5): 646–666.

Ranstorp, M. 2009. "Mapping terrorism studies after 9/11, An academic field of old problems and new prospects." In: Jackson, R. *et al.* (eds.) *Critical Terrorism Studies, A new research agenda.* Oxon: Routledge: 13–33.

Ryan, L., Elenore, K., and Ludovica, B. 2009. "Muslim Youth in Barnet: Exploring Identity, Citizenship and Belonging locally and in the Wider Context", *London: Social Policy Research* Centre. Available at: https://eprints.mdx.ac.uk/5093/1/Ryan_Muslim_Youth_in_Barnet_executive_summary.pdf

Sabir, R. 2011. "I Won Terror Compensation, but My Struggle for Justice Continues." *The Guardian.* Available at: http://www.guardian.co.uk/commentisfree/2011/sep/19/terrorcompensation-olice-university

Slack, J. 2011. "40 UK Universities Are Now Breeding Grounds for Terror as Hard Line Groups Peddle Hate on Campus", *Mail Online.* Available online at: http://www.dailymail.co.uk/news/article-1394625/40-UK-universities-breeding-grounds-terror.html

Simcox, R., Stuart, H., and Ahmed, H. 2010. "Islamist Terrorism: The British Connections", *The Centre for Social Cohesion.* Available online at: http://www.socialcohesion.co.uk/uploads/1278089320islamist_terrorism_preview.pdf

Universities UK. 2011. "Freedom of Speech on Campus: Rights and Responsibilities in UK Universities." Available online at http://www.universitiesuk.ac.uk/Publications/Documents/FreedomOfSpeechOnCampusRightsAndResponsibilitiesInUKuniversities.pdf

Yaqoob, S. 2008. "Government's PVE agenda is failing to tackle extremism", *The Muslim News.* Available at: http://www.muslimnews.co.uk/paper/index.php?article=3795

CHAPTER 4

# Surveillance and the 'Monitoring' of Citizens by the State

**Abstract** This chapter discusses monitoring and the surveillance techniques and theoretical approaches that have been used to examine the process. Our focus is the actualisation of the Prevent Strategy, in itself a form of monitoring and surveillance, where those in authority record the activities of students and make decisions on their interpretations of the 'risk' credential of their students. Furthermore, the widespread application of monitoring and surveillance techniques has been posited to cause a number of socially dangerous consequences which stem from its ability to discriminate between different population groups within its multifarious domains of application (see Gandy, Ethics Inf Technol 12(1): 29–42, 2010). Surveillance, per se, can be understood as an organising principle which relies on the observation of a domain, and the data resulting from that observation is then used to enable regulation, governance, or management (Lyon, Surveillance society: monitoring everyday life. Open University Press, Buckingham, 2001: 2). The Prevent Strategy gives rise, reason, and authority to, how, as we argue, institutions such as universities monitor their charges and perform roles of surveillance by monitoring students for evidence of radicalisation or terrorist intent. We do, however, remain attentive to the necessary workings of monitoring; for instance, private sector and governing authorities at all levels of scale rely on surveillant techniques to control the risks associated with their activities. The chapter offers an overview of the theoretical underpinnings of monitoring

 
I. Awan et al., *Terrorism in the Classroom*, Palgrave Studies in Risk, Crime and Society,
https://doi.org/10.1007/978-3-030-01710-1_4

and the agendas that inform the Prevent Strategy applied in an educational context; as the chapter progresses, we discuss concepts of bureaucracy and technology, risk control, and responsibilisation in furthering our thoughts.

**Keywords** Surveillance • Monitoring • Consequences • Theoretical approach • Universities

## Introduction

In this chapter we draw upon the theoretical approaches used when examining processes of monitoring and surveillance. Our focus is the Prevent Strategy, in itself a form of monitoring and surveillance, where those in authority record the activities of students and make decisions on their interpretations of the 'risk' posed towards and by students. It is in this context that we consider how the widespread application of monitoring and surveillance techniques has been applied to cause a number of socially dangerous consequences which stem from its ability to discriminate between different population groups (see Gandy 2010). Surveillance, per se, can be understood as an organising principle which relies on the observation of a domain, and the data resulting from that observation is then used to enable regulation, governance, or management (Lyon 2001). As we have seen in Chaps. 2 and 3, the CTSA, CONTEST, and Prevent Strategy give rise, reason, and authority to how institutions such as universities monitor their charges and their students for evidence of radicalisation, extremism, or terrorist intent. We do, however, remain attentive to the necessary workings of monitoring; for instance, private sector and governing authorities at all levels of scale rely on surveillant techniques to run their organisations. The chapter therefore offers an overview of the theoretical underpinnings to surveillance and how these might be applied in an educational context as the chapter progresses, we discuss concepts of bureaucracy and technology, risk control, and responsibilisation in furthering our thoughts.

## Bureaucracy and Technology

The study of surveillance to date has (rightly) focused on documenting the discriminatory consequences and local practices of surveillance. This has resulted in calls from a number of academic positions to render surveillance systems more accountable and transparent given their discriminatory consequences (PATS project 2011; Surveillance Studies Network 2006). Indeed, this is the central ethical concern of surveillance studies and forms the backbone of the field. Surveillance's ability to 'socially sort' populations (Lyon 2001) into databases has discriminatory consequences for populations deemed risky (Vlcek 2007) or of less economic value (Gandy 2010) and results in varying levels of convenience, access to services, use of space, and differential life chances, amongst other things (Graham 2005; Surveillance Studies Network 2006). Studies of institutions (Lianos 2003; Hasslebladh and Kallinikos 2000; Bennett 2001) further emphasise the idiosyncratic nature of surveillance and the contested nature of information codification within organisations—where advantages are relayed to particular populations. Notable studies such as Gilliom's (2001), Thompson and Genosko's (2009), and Ericson and Haggerty's (1997) also do much to uncover the organising processes surrounding surveillance in different institutional settings. Elsewhere, Ball (2002) highlights how different elements of surveillance may be connected, and, most significantly, Haggerty and Ericson (2000) highlight how a 'surveillant assemblage' of interconnected elements combines as local instances of surveillance are connected. The nature of that connection is the relationship between the many different types of agency is an 'invisible infrastructure' aided by technological development and the speed and efficiency of data collection. Just think of how digital data collection and analysis has changed policing, for instance, ANPR (Automatic Number Plate Recognition), a plethora of cameras littering UK route ways that record each car that passes them. This information is often used to plot the movements of specific individuals.

Various forms of technology have aided in the accumulation of information, and as Deleuze contests, 'types of machines are easily matched with each type of society – not that machines are determining, but because they express those social forms capable of generating them and using them' (1992: 6). Deleuze's suggestion is that the social and cultural imperative to technology is telling to our understandings of the techno-social process. We design technology with purpose to perform the tasks we require. The bureaucratic imperative that Weber (1983) once spoke of is realised by the technologies which enable it. Yet, the well-tread dilemma that security and liberty are traded against or off each other (De Hert 2005; Waldron 2003) is pressing within such arguments. Technologies may enable greater 'freedoms' and sharing of information, but they also serve to record sensitive information on an unprecedented scale (see Bauman and Lyon 2013). Lianos (2003) continues a similar charge when examining the mechanisms of control—for him it is not simply about the winners and losers of surveillance and surveillance technologies. As he warns, the normality of social control and its technological bearings are often straightforward and non-eventful.

> [I]n the majority of cases, a context or a device of institutional normativity does not involve any attempt to structure the internal premises of user behaviour. ... An ATM, that is to say a banking network, does not ask if the user is a legitimate client but compares a series of numbers (the 'PIN code') with stored information. So long as the match is assured, the transaction is authorised. What the subject thinks, does or believes, is irrelevant to what the institution controls; it is simply meaningless for the technological device. (Lianos 2003: 423)

There is, as he continues, a politics in the 'birth, survival and proliferation' of technologies, as well as in the surveillant intent or functionality of those technologies. An example of this could be the many UK governmental funding calls asking for technological responses to the Prevent Strategy, the clear objective being the production of a digital or technological device or platform that will aid the implementation of the programme (see Innovate 2015, 2016). And this is a key indicator as to how the government is viewing potential solutions to countering terrorism. Dodge and Kitchen (2005) explore some of the tensions in relation to coding and categorisation. As they suggest, barcodes commonly found on commodities and other items attempt to remove the messiness of life in a 'trajectory... towards a machine-readable world' (2005: 878). It is the concept of order that facilitates speed and technology by permitting, in this case, life to be structured by an authority grounded in the machine. The emphasis here is classification and the generation of information (Bowker and Starr 1999). As Dodge and Kitchin suggest, the corporeal clues of old (the handshake, the development of face-to-face trust, etc.) have been removed.

Industry, science, and new communications have played a dramatic role in combatting potential national security risks (Lyon and Zureik 1996; Bigo 2001; Levi and Wall 2004; Zureik 2004; Wilson 2006). Lyon (2001, 2002) argues surveillance and the technologies it employs remain critical to everyday lives and the world we live in. Surveillance Studies has in the past looked to various aspects of change and technological development, notable amongst these being how surveillance has developed across domains (see Haggerty and Ericson 2000; Ball 2002; Gad and Lauritsen 2009)—and, indeed, the 'commonalities between each of these surveilled spaces' (Ball 2002: 580). Ball argues there are elements that can help to frame the nature of increasingly abundant surveillances and their interactions with end-users. Moreover, Marx (2002) offers historical comparisons of change and the increasingly sophisticated and comprehensive methods of data collection. Momentous events also produce change; for example, within two weeks of the 2005 London bombings the then British Prime Minister Tony Blair introduced 12 new counter-terrorism measures (see Cobain 2010). Added to this could be instances such as the Amber Rudd (then UK Home Secretary) response to a terrorist attack, where she stated all WhatsApp messages should not be encrypted to allow the security forces to intercept potential attacks (see Huffington Post 2017). Our intention here is to consider the momentum and trajectory of social reactions to the diffusion of governmental strategies that monitor certain populations and how this is actioned and understood by those expected to participate in new modes of monitoring.

## Risk Control

Monitoring is rarely linear; it is complicated and incorporates a host of variety. Indeed the very remit of Prevent is, as we have argued, ambiguous (see Spiller et al. 2018). Structure and agency have been used by social theorists as a means of expanding explorations of just how the 'social realities' of initiatives such as security interventions can be comprehended. Structure can be viewed as the rules, regulations, and organisational patterns that constitute institutions and work groups. Agency on the other hand is how human actors sit within these patterns. As Deleuze and Guattari (1994: 131) state, 'a science must give order to the chaos of life, whereas the task of philosophy is to think and confront chaos'. Our emphasis continues in this spirit, and we are conscious of the emerging security reality, one built on manipulated parameters or even virtual realties—for instance, how university lecturers, doctors, or primary school teachers are expected to perform security roles. Other theorists have also considered notions of order and chaos; for example, Bourdieu (1977, 1984) suggests a notion of habitus, which in effect is a 'structuring structure' where the individual/agent engages in predictable practices that for

Bourdieu sustain hierarchies (Dowding 2008). Habitus, to some extent, uses structure and agency as a method of reviewing how rules are followed, and as Chouinard (1997: 364) suggests, 'human agency is seen as being shaped by both social structure and conditions of daily life'. Yet, much of this work and others hold firm to the dualities that create the interaction between structure and agency, in that both are seen as distinctive domains in exploring social 'reality'. This is not to discredit some of this work, and indeed, the duality of structure and agent is essential in framing this analysis; however, what we propose is that the ambiguity and tensions are central to how actors, especially university lecturers, interpret the rules of Prevent.

Discourses, languages, interactions, bodies, randomness, thoughts, ideas, or hermeneutics are the lifeblood to how counter-terrorism measures are performed and indeed how surveillance often functions. While digitally assisted technologies such as algorithms may locate 'risk' or anomalies, ultimately accountability lies with those responsibilised to take action. It is human actors who are responsible; it is they who scour for 'non-obvious relationships between pieces of data in large input data sets, or to look for unusual patterns of behaviour' (Canhoto and Backhouse 2007: 409). There is an interesting dynamic between something like technology and an actant; for instance, as Latour discusses, the dynamics of the machine and agent can often present moments of confusion and absurdity, particularly when machines enjoy tangible qualities. Latour (1996: 210–11) details such a moment when Norbert (a character in his more novelistic passages) confronts technology:

> He routinely thanked the automatic ticket machines at highway toll booths. He queried automatic tellers at banks about communication problems. He had long conversations with electric staplers. He noted the degree of politeness, laziness, violence, or nastiness of all the automatic door openers he came across, going so far as to tip them, which usually left them quite indifferent.

Latour's observations advocate the anthropomorphic qualities of technologies, and while the thoughts of tipping a door seem ludicrous, it does offer the question of why objects become animated. For instance, why and how they are allowed to 'speak' or inscribe reality, reliability, knowledge, and power. It is in these terms we highlight the power of technology and the reliance on technology in identifying risk and categories, creating rules and helping to order chaos and risk. In this context, the training of staff, the management of organisations, and the activities of organisation become real or practised. Sewell and Barker (2006) are keen to suggest there is rationality in how life is organised, and that with the ever-growing reliance on technology, lives become increasingly controlled and predictable (see Lyon 2007; Vlcek 2007). Yet, confusion reigns as to how it is enacted by those responsibilised, and as we will see in Chap. 7, particularly by HE staff.

## The Responsibilisation of Citizens

The rise of a neoliberal agenda which seeks to responsibilise non-state actors for security has been to the fore in recent commentaries on security (see Goold et al. 2010; Loader and Walker 2010). Indeed, much of this work has called for greater understanding of new political economies of security (White 2011; Huysmans 2011) and UK governmental initiatives, such as *Prevent* (2009), *Contest* (2011), or *Request a Check* (see Home Office 2014), that encourage 'special' actors to participate in security roles. Key to the rationale that drives such momentum is a compliance towards the security objectives and new powers of security responsibility. Garland (1996) has argued for appreciations of 'governance-at-a-distance'—the state, as he suggests, cannot do it alone. Therefore, strategies of responsibilisation involve multiple agencies, actors, and organisations in order to reduce crime. This can take the shape of activities such as media participation and poster campaigns or through 'self-help' groups such as Neighbourhood Watch. This work which has become somewhat dated, particularly with the advent of digital capture, does, however, lend itself to the antecedents of the principles that underpin the Prevent Strategy—namely, the enrolment of private actors in new modes of governing crime or more aptly countering terrorism, extremism, and radicalisation.

The significance of new security responsibilities has been examined at state level (Adey 2012) and in relation to activities such as airline travel (Bennett 2005). Indeed, in a climate where increasingly non-security specialist organisations are implicated in national security regimes, this is an important conceptual development in the impact and enrolment of university staff—it poses questions to the political and indeed labour expectation that the strategy demands. Premised on much of the political mire of post-9/11, Iraq, and now Syria, there is a deliberate and sustained focus on certain populations that have been deemed risky (Aradau and

Van Munster 2007; Heath-Kelly 2013; see also Chap. 3). Much like the focuses of the past, where those deemed to be part of community involved in terror receive added attention, see the Irish 'problem' (McGovern and Tobin 2010). In this instance, religious and political identities become targeted by association. As a result, levels of monitoring towards those perceived as a risk increase. This can be best understood when an activity deemed to pose a risk rationalises the choices or opportunities for those moderated as risky (Surveillance Studies Network 2010). This can have the effect that any non-conventional activity becomes muted or mundane, and innocuous activities, such as student debates, are curtailed or censored (Independent 2016).

What may also be drawn from the literature here is the role of the assessor and how someone like a university lecturer is equipped to make a security decision. In similar circumstances, work on whistle-blowers has questioned what gives them the right to make the decision to publicise the critical information (Kagiaros 2015; Moberly 2018). The parallel we draw is how the whistle-blower may make the informed decision to render that the information discovered is of 'public interest', and for the lecturer, it is to decide if a person of interest is of sufficient risk. The question remains if the whistle-blowers are the most informed person to make the decision. Equally, governmental unease with universities can also be viewed in the actions of Tory whip Chris Heaton-Harris who wrote to every university vice chancellor, seeking a list of all courses and professors teaching on issues related to Brexit (see Guardian 2017a)—his motives in doing so remain unclear; however, we feel it is fair to presume Heaton-Harris had concerns about how Brexit was being portrayed to students. His actions have been viewed with universal disdain by academic staff (BBC 2018).

## Prevent Literature in Education

The responsibilisation of new actors with the Prevent Strategy is contentious and has stimulated critique on 'risk work', 'British Values' (now a central element to the British educational curriculum), and the idea of being a responsible citizen (as discussed in Chap. 3). The realities of 'risk work' and what this entails have moved the debate towards a more empirical overview of what the strategy entails. Indeed, much of this new work is keen to emphasise the unintended or averse consequence of the strategy on those who are ultimately the front-line workers or enforcers of Prevent. Stanley et al. (2018: 136) stress the 'multiple interpretive possibilities' as to how the strategy is understood. Key here is the multiagency context of the work, where teams are working in conjunction with others, that is, social workers working with counter-terrorism police. Stanley et al.'s findings question how the Prevent Strategy was imposed on social workers, where they had to respond to issues of 'radicalisation risk'. The Prevent Strategy, they argue, ignores that people can be radical in non-violent ways, and as a result set a percussive agenda towards those that may be practising open dialogue, and indeed acting within their democratic rights. A theme to emerge from Stanley et al.'s (2018) work was the lack of a multiagency model—there was a lack of transparency and knowledge sharing amongst organisations working to counter terrorism. As Stanley et al. highlight, often those who have worked on cases were not informed of the final outcomes of their work, thus hindering the potential to establish best practice workers remained uninformed of results from cases they had been reported, and therefore establishing best practice becomes challenging. Moreover, mistakes have been made when identifying radicalisation, for instance, gang-related activities referred to as radicalisation.

Miscommunication and defensive reporting are a common thread in the literature,—where individuals report on matters due to a fear of prosecution. Examples could include non-violent critiques of 'British Values' and potentials for this to be construed as dangerous and reportable (see Grace 2018). There is an ongoing and tension-filled narrative on 'British Values' and the presumptions around particular expectations of national identities and religions as well as resulting relationships with state, teachers, and education per se (see Elton-Chalcraft et al. 2017), unlike, for instance, the USA, where a very clear projection is evident; reinforced when most, if not all, schools swear allegiance to the American flag each morning. For British schools and society, a conventional narrative is less discernible. The emphasis in British society has been on an assimilationist model, and in the post-war years, emphasis has been on vulnerability and loss of identity with the influx of new migration (Peach 1999). Yet, particularly in a post-9/11 context, problems persist in multicultural and non-assimilationist models (see Sears et al. 2011; Garner 2012). In this regard, educational organisations are a central and formative platform for highlighting a cohesiveness to how an implied Britishness is taught, understood, and valued. Elton-Chalcraft et al.'s (2017) work echoes the crux of what we are chasing here, in that there is a clear sense that teachers and trainee teachers are being persuaded by bureaucratic oversight, such as Ofsted (the inspectorate and regulator of schools in the UK), that promotes a clear warning that if one fails to comply with the directives of the programme, then there will be repercussions. This is similar to how industries, organisations, or sectors such as banking (see Ball et al. 2015) or health NHS (see Heath-Kelly and Strausz 2018) have been mandated and accepted extra security responsibilities. Common amongst all this is the curtailing of a critical challenge as to how such compliances are being indicated and indeed understood by those at the 'front-line'. What may be missed here are the understandings of the ethical, racial, religious inequality or other features that fundamentally position relations between teacher, pupil, and student teacher in the classroom (Mirza and Meetoo 2012). These are important contributors to how people understand their roles and respond to such directives.

Some recent work has also questioned the responsibilisation of educators in the Prevent Strategy, amongst which has been Thomas's (2017) observations on Prevent as a policy that counters the community cohesion impetus of pre-9/11 governmental initiatives. His argument centres on the idea that events such as the Bradford riots helped to formalise notions of governmental favouritism towards non-white populations (see Cantle and Thomas 2014; Denham 2001). Policy aimed at halting racial inequalities succeeded in raising tensions amongst different populations. This originates from 'resource-envy' (Thomas 2017: 5), where particular groups gain access to governmental funding streams. Despite such tensions, Thomas's focus is undoubtedly on 'risky' and 'at risk' communities (see Heath-Kelly 2013), and he suggests responsibilisation is a 'communitarianist' issue. A concept based on the fact that individuals will or should intervene is the face of wrongdoing or when certain groups become violent extremists. The emphasis is on social policy or social movement, much influenced by Giddens's (1998) 'third way'. Giddens attests 'we need to more actively accept responsibilities for the consequences of what we do and the lifestyle habits we adopt' (Giddens 1998: 37). We are not entirely sure Thomas is correct here and feel he has complicated notions of the citizen and the state's role in what citizens do. Giddens suggests 'we' are responsible for what we do and therefore Thomas is right to draw on the responsibilities placed at the individual's door; for example, if we eat more junk food our chances of obesity or diabetes increase, and this is something the individual should be aware of because it is directly related to them. However, we disagree with this as a communitarianist agenda, as this is not something demanded or enshrined by the state. Instead, governmental campaigns or institutions such as the NHS seek to highlight and promote the dangers of unwise eating habits. The Prevent Strategy, we would suggest, pushes responsibilisation not in a communitarianist ideal but in a neoliberal manner, where the emphasis is to be proactive, decentralised, and cost-effective. Further complications could include challenges to staff's pastoral roles when exposed to confidential information, or indeed for impressionable young adults whose notions of finding an identity, or expressing themselves, joining groups, or to some degree policing themselves to perform and act in ways that are acceptable to peer groups can instil conformity and self-monitoring (Bailey and Steeves 2013; Andrejevic 2009). This, as Marwick (2012) would contend, is 'social surveillance' where it is the masses who watch the masses, rather than a single overseer who monitors and influences those under its charge.

Within UK educational organisations, there are growing examples where academic or functional activities have been co-opted to work with the Prevent Strategy. As *The Guardian* (2017b) reports, students using university computers have been warned their online activities are being monitored 'to aid the process of preventing people being drawn into terrorism'. A university notice to students states, 'You must not create, download, store or transmit unlawful material or material that is indecent, offensive, defamatory, threatening, discriminatory or extremist. The university reserves the right to block or monitor access to such material'. Indeed, within our very own institution there are Prevent 'friendly' computers, where if your work involves reviewing terrorist materials or information on groups such as ISIS, then one must apply to use a machine that is registered to be used in such settings. Equally one could apply other everyday activities such as the security swipe cards used to enter and leave building, library records, IT firewalls, or attendance records, all of which have the potential to monitor the activities of staff and students at educational organisations. This, as McGovern (2016) argues, is representative of and in accordance with the well-established principles of governmental targets. School league tables, NHS waiting times, or Ofsted reports, phenomena all public organisations are more than familiar with, are indicators of esteem (or failure) and set the template for how UK organisation should be run. Therefore, recording data to evidence the competences of an organisation readily transfer to measures such as the Prevent Strategy. Added to this could be the requirements placed on universities to monitor Tier 4 students—those from outside the EEA with visas to study. Universities which perform their tasks effectively are rewarded with special status by the visa-issuing governmental agencies (Dear 2018). Undoubtedly, tasks of monitoring students are essential to education, for example, keeping records of exam results; however, monitoring and surveillance tasks that are not based on traditional educational models are harder to comprehend and accept (Mattsson and Säljö 2018). Extremism, radicalisation, and terrorism are just three of these agendas that have encroached into the educational sector and, as Chap. 7 discusses, are problematic for the university staff we spoke to.

## Conclusion

In this chapter we have highlighted some of the opportunities and previous work that has examined aspects of monitoring. Important to our discussion is gaining an understanding of just how we can make sense of movements towards 'extra' watching, recording, and analysis of people in educational contexts. What can we learn from this, and indeed what can we learn of the consequences of asking those in positions of civil authority to surveil their charges for potential misdeeds? As we have seen, the work we highlight covers a critical perspective to surveillance, and this is intentional as this is our perspective. However, as mentioned, we remain conscious of the organising principles that are at the heart of all organisations—levels of hierarchy, bureaucracy, or record-keeping are a necessity to the smooth running of any organisation. Where we take exception, and indeed as much of the work cited suggests, is when the monitoring contributes to inequalities, lack of transparency, or ill-conceived consequences—or quite simply is not effective in what it was intended to do. Much like the hopes that were once extended to the introduction of CCTV where it would substantially aid the eradication of crime, in fact, evidence suggests CCTV does little to prevent crime (Webster 2009). This specific argument may be misguided in applying to the Prevent Strategy, as there have been clear cases where it has helped in the fight against extremism. However, what does remain questionable is the excessive nature of asking entire organisations to monitor entire student populations for possible offences or, as we have seen in Chap. 3, by using rules, regulations, and instructions based on phrasing that remains ambiguous and poorly understood by those mandated to enact the guidance. In Chap. 5, we build upon our critical perspective and review the governmental mandate with the legislation of the Prevent Strategy in HE.

## References

Adey, P. 2012. "Borders, identification and surveillance: New regimes of border control". In Ball, K, K Haggerty and D Lyon (eds.) *Routledge Handbook of Surveillance Studies*. London: Routledge: 193–200.

Andrejevic, M. 2009. *iSpy: Surveillance and power in the interactive era*. Kanas: University of Kansas Press.

Aradau, C., & Van Munster, R. 2007. "Governing terrorism through risk: Taking precautions, (un) knowing the future", *European journal of international relations, 13*(1): 89–115.

Bailey, J. and Steeves, V. 2013. "Will the real digital girl please stand up?: Examining the gap between policy dialogue and girls' accounts of their digital existence". In Macgregor Wise, J. and Koskela, H. (eds.) *New Visualities, New Technologies: the New Ecstasy of Communication*. Burlington: Ashgate: 41–65.

Ball K. 2002. "Elements of surveillance: a new framework and future directions", *Information, Communication and Society*, 5(4): 573–590.

Ball, K., Canhoto, A., Daniel, E., Dibb, S., Meadows, M. & Spiller, K. 2015. The *Private Security State?: Surveillance, consumer Data and the War on Terror*. Copenhagen: Copenhagen Business School Press.

Bauman, Z., & Lyon, D. 2013. *Liquid surveillance: A conversation*. Cambridge: Polity Press.

BBC. 2018. "How universities replied to that Brexit letter". Available at https://www.bbc.co.uk/news/education-42431780

Bennett J, 2001. *The Enchantment of Modern Life: Attachments, Crossings and Ethics*. Princeton, N.J.: Princeton University Press.

Bennett, C. J. 2005. "What happens when you book an airline ticket? The collection and processing of passenger data post-9/11". In Zureik, E. and Salter, M. (eds.) *Global surveillance and policing*. Devon: Willian Publishing: 113–38.

Bigo, D. 2001. "The Mobius ribbon of internal and external securities". In Albert, M., Jacobson, D. and Lapid, Y. (eds.) *Identities, Borders, Orders*. Minneapolis, M.N.: University of Minnesota Press: 91–116.

Bourdieu, P. 1977. *Outline of a theory of practice*. Cambridge: Cambridge University Press.

Bourdieu, P. 1984. *Distinction: A social critique of the judgement of taste*. Abingdon: Routledge.

Bowker, G. and Star, S. 1999. *Sorting Things Out: Classification and its consequences*. Cambridge, M.A.: MIT Press.

Canhoto, A. and Backhouse, J. 2007. "Profiling under conditions of ambiguity: An application in the financial services industry", *Journal of Retailing and Consumer Services*, 14: 408–419.

Cantle, T. and Thomas, P. 2014. *Taking the Think Project Forward: The Need for Preventative Anti-Extremism Educational Work*. Swansea: Ethnic Youth Support Team.

Cobain I. 2010. "London bombings: the day the anti-terrorism rules changed", *The Guardian*. Available at: https://www.theguardian.com/uk/2010/jul/07/london-bombings-anti-terrorism

Chouinard, V. 1997. "Structure and Agency: contested concepts in human geography", *The Canadian Geographer*, 41(4): 363–377.

Dear, L. 2018. "The University as Border Control", *International Education Journal: Comparative Perspectives*, 17(1): 7–23.

De Hert, P. 2005. "Balancing security and liberty within the European human rights framework. A critical reading of the Court's case law in the light of surveillance and criminal law enforcement strategies after 9/11", *Utrecht L. Rev.*, *1*: 68–98.

Deleuze, G. 1992. "Postscript on the Societies of Control", October 59: 3–7.

Deleuze, G. and Guattari, F. 1994. *What is philosophy?* London: Verso.

Denham, J. 2001. *Building Cohesive Communities: A Report of the Ministerial Group on Public Order and Community Cohesion*. London: Home Office.

Dodge, M. and Kitchen, R. 2005. "Codes of Life: identification codes and the machine-readable world", *Environment and Planning D: Society and Space*, 23: 851–881.

Dowding, K. 2008. "Agency and structure: Interpreting power relationships", *Journal of Power*, 1(1): 21–36.

Elton-Chalcraft, S., Lander, V., Revell, L., Warner, D., & Whitworth, L. 2017. "To promote, or not to promote fundamental British values? Teachers' standards, diversity and teacher education", *British Educational Research Journal*, *43*(1): 29–48.

Gad, C. and Lauritsen, P. 2009. "Situated Surveillance: an ethnographic study of fisheries inspection in Denmark", *Surveillance & Society*, 7(1): 49–57.

Gandy, O. 2010. "Engaging Rational Discrimination: Exploring Reasons for Placing Regulatory Constraints on Decision Support Systems", *Ethics and Information Technology*, 12(1): 29–42.

Garland, D. 1996. "The Limits of the Sovereign State: strategies of Crime Control in Contemporary Society", *The British Journal of Criminology*, 36(4): 445–471.

Garner, S. 2012. "A moral economy of whiteness: Behaviours, belonging and Britishness", *Ethnicities*, 12(4): 445–464.

Giddens, A. 1998. *The Third Way*. Cambridge: Polity.

Gilliom, J. 2001. *Overseers of the Poor: Surveillance, Resistance, and the Limits of Privacy*. Chicago: University of Chicago Press.

Goold, B., Loader, I. and Thumala, A. 2010. "Consuming security? Tools for a sociology of security Consumption", *Theoretical Criminology*, 14(3): 3–30.

Grace, J. 2018. "Countering extremism and recording dissent: Intelligence analysis and the Prevent agenda in UK Higher Education", *Journal of Information Rights, Policy and Practice*, 2(2): 1–10.

Graham S. D. N., 2005. "Software-sorted geographies", *Progress in Human Geography*, 29(5): 562–580.

Guardian. 2017a. "Universities deplore 'McCarthyism' as MP demands list of tutors lecturing on Brexit". Available at: https://www.theguardian.com/education/2017/oct/24/universities-mccarthyism-mp-demands-list-brexit-chris-heaton-harris

Guardian. 2017b. "London university tells students their emails may be monitored". Available at: https://www.theguardian.com/uk-news/2017/jan/20/university-warns-students-emails-may-be-monitored-kings-college-london-prevent

Ericson, R. V., Ericson, R. V., & Haggerty, K. D. 1997. *Policing the risk society.* Toronto: University of Toronto Press.

Haggerty, K. and Ericson, R. 2000. "The surveillant assemblage", *The British Journal of Sociology*, 51(4): 605–622.

Hasslebladh, H. and Kallinikos, J. 2000. "The Project of Rationalization: A Critique and Reappraisal of Neo-Institutionalism in Organization Studies", Organization Studies, 21(4): 697–720.

Heath-Kelly, C. 2013. "Counter-terrorism and the counterfactual: Producing the 'radicalisation' discourse and the UK PREVENT strategy", *The British journal of politics and international relations*, 15(3): 394–415.

Heath-Kelly, C. and Strausz, E 2018. "Counterterrorism in the NHS: Evaluating Prevent Duty Safeguarding". Available at https://www.docdroid.net/boB68fG/counter-terrorism-in-the-nhs.pdf

Home Office. 2014. *Request a Check.* Available at https://eforms.homeoffice.gov.uk/outreach/righttowork.ofml

Huffington Post. 2017. "'Completely Unacceptable' We Can't See Terrorists' WhatsApp Messages, Says Amber Rudd". Available at: https://www.huffingtonpost.co.uk/entry/amber-rudd-whatsapp-terrorists_uk_58d7978fe4b0378 7d3595d1f

Huysmans, J. 2011. "What's in an act? On security speech acts and little security nothings", *Security Dialogue*, 42(4–5): 371–383.

Independent. 2016. "Censorship at Edinburgh University 'out of control', says student". Available at: https://www.independent.co.uk/student/news/censorship-at-edinburgh-university-out-of-control-says-student-a6980311.html

Innovate. 2015. "Innovation Fund for Prevent". Available at: https://sbri.innovateuk.org/competition-display-page/-/asset_publisher/E809e7RZ5ZTz/content/innovation-fund-for-prevent/1524978

Innovate. 2016. "Radicalisation and Terrorism Funding: Apply for Funding". Available at: https://www.gov.uk/government/news/radicalisation-and-terrorism-prevention-apply-for-funding

Kagiaros, D. 2015. "Protecting 'national security' whistleblowers in the Council of Europe: an evaluation of three approaches on how to balance national security with freedom of expression", *The International Journal of Human Rights*, 19(4): 408–428.

Latour B. 1996. *Aramis or the Love of Technology.* Harvard University Press, M.A.: Cambridge.

Levi, M. and Wall, D. S. 2004. "Technologies, Security, and Privacy in the Post-9/11 European Information Society", *Journal of Law and Society*, 31(2): 194–220.

Lianos, M. 2003. "Social Control after Foucault", Surveillance & Society, 1(3): 412–30.

Loader, I. and Walker, N. 2010. *Civilising Security.* Cambridge: Cambridge University Press.

Lyon, D. 2001. *Surveillance Society: Monitoring Everyday Life.* Buckingham: Open University Press.

Lyon, D. 2002. "Everyday Surveillance: Personal data and social classifications", *Information, Communication and Society*, 5(2): 242–257.

Lyon, D. 2007. *Surveillance Studies: An Overview.* Cambridge: Polity Press.

Lyon, D. and Zureik, E. 1996. "Surveillance, privacy, and the new technology". In D Lyon and E Zureik (eds.) *Computers, surveillance, and privacy.* University of Minnesota Press, Minneapolis, M.N.: 1–18.

Marwick, A. E. 2012. "The public domain: Social surveillance in everyday life", *Surveillance & Society*, 9(4): 378–393.

Marx, G. T. 2002. "What's New About the "New Surveillance"? Classifying for Change and Continuity", *Surveillance & Society*, 1(1): 9–29.

Mattsson, C., & Säljö, R. 2018. "Violent extremism, national security and prevention. Institutional discourses and their implications for schooling", *British Journal of Educational Studies*, 66(1): 109–125.

McGovern, M. 2016. "The university, Prevent and cultures of compliance". *Prometheus*, 34(1): 49–62.

McGovern, M. and Tobin, A. 2010. Countering Terror or Counter-Productive: Comparing Irish and British Muslim Experiences of Counter-insurgency Law and Policy. Project Report. Edge Hill University, Ormskirk.

Mirza, H. S. & Meetoo, V. 2012. *Respecting Difference: Race, Faith and Culture for Teacher Educators.* Institute of Education-London: London.

Moberly, R. 2018. "Confidentiality and Whistleblowing", *North Carolina Law Review*, 96(3): 751–788.

PATS project. 2011. "Privacy Awareness through Security Organisation Branding". Available at http://www.pats-project.eu/.

Peach, C. 1999. "London and New York: contrasts in British and American models of segregation with a comment by Nathan Glazer", *International Journal of Population Geography*, 5(5): 319–347.

Sears, A., Davies, I., & Reid, A. D. 2011. "From Britishness to nothingness and back again: Looking for a way forward in citizenship education". In Mycock, A and McGlynn, C (eds.) *Britishness, identity and citizenship: the view from abroad.* Bern: Peter Lang: 291–312.

Sewell G, and Barker, J. 2006. "Coercion Versus Care: Using Irony To Make Sense Of Organisational Surveillance", *Academy of Management Review*, 31(4): 934–961.

Spiller, K., Awan, I., & Whiting, A. (2018). "'What does terrorism look like?': University lecturers' interpretations of their Prevent duties and tackling extremism in UK universities", *Critical Studies on Terrorism*, 11(1): 130–150.

Stanley, T., Guru, S., & Gupta, A. 2018. "Working with prevent: Social work options for cases of 'radicalisation risk'", *Practice*, 30(2): 131–146.

Surveillance Studies Network. 2006. "A Report on the Surveillance Society", *Surveillance Studies Network.* Available at: https://ico.org.uk/media/about-the-ico/documents/1042390/surveillance-society-full-report-2006.pdf

Surveillance Studies Network. 2010. *An Update to a report on the surveillance society UK Information Commissioner.* Wilmslow: Information Commissioner's Office.

Thomas, P. 2017. "Changing experiences of responsibilisation and contestation within counter-terrorism policies: the British Prevent experience", *Policy & Politics*, 45(3): 305–321.

Thompson, S. and Genosko, G. 2009. *Punched Drunk: Alcohol, Surveillance and the LCBO 1927–1975.* Nova Scotia: Fernwood.

Vlcek, W. 2007. "Surveillance to combat Terrorist Financing in Europe: Whose Liberty, Whose Security", *European* Studies, 16(1): 99–119.

Waldron, J. 2003. "Security and liberty: The image of balance", *Journal of Political Philosophy*, 11(2): 191–210.

Weber, M. 1983. *Max Weber on capitalism, bureaucracy, and religion: a selection of texts.* Allen & Unwin Australia.

Webster, C. W. R. 2009. "CCTV policy in the UK: reconsidering the evidence base", *Surveillance and Society*, 6(1): 10–22.

White, A. 2011. "The new political economy of private security", *Theoretical Criminology*, 16(1): 85–101.

Wilson, D. 2006. "Biometrics, Borders and the Ideal Suspect". In S Pickering and L Weber (eds.) *Borders, mobility and technologies of* control. Dordrecht: Springer: 87–109.

Zureik E. 2004. "Governance, Security and Technology: The Case of Biometrics", *Studies in Political Economy*, 73(1): 113–137.

CHAPTER 5

# Governmentality and Managing Security Risks

**Abstract** After briefly exploring different theoretical models of power, this chapter provides an overview of the radical model of power put forward by Michel Foucault, placing a specific focus on his 'third modality'—*governmentality*. The chapter moves on to demonstrate how the Prevent Duty operates as an extension of a broader strategy of neoliberal governance that seeks to manage the population through an encroachment of the national security agenda into sections of civil society such as education. To demonstrate how this has been achieved, the chapter discusses how the productive discourses of radicalisation, vulnerability, and resilience work within (and constitute) a 'dispositif of precautionary risk' to contribute towards the entrenchment of a particular 'risk knowledge', elevating it to the status of truth and legitimising this unprecedented expansion of counter-terrorism powers into education. The chapter concludes by arguing that this expansion, which has been presented as 'common sense' and necessary, is instead a worrying development directed at a section of the population and motivated by an enhanced ability to manage potential risks that puts further strain on already stretched practitioners, limits expression and thought within education, and broadens notion of suspicious populations to include students and young people.

**Keywords** Governmentality • Power • Foucault • Precaution • Risk

 
I. Awan et al., *Terrorism in the Classroom*, Palgrave Studies in Risk, Crime and Society,
https://doi.org/10.1007/978-3-030-01710-1_5

## Introduction

The Prevent Duty has meant that educational institutions have had to take on a counter-terrorism function as a statutory requirement. As we saw in the previous chapter, this has manifested in the creation of new disciplinary practices and forms of surveillance being deployed within spaces of education. In this chapter we shift the focus from a disciplinary analysis and consider how the Duty provides a contemporary development in a broader strategy of *governmentality* that has sought to categorise and manage sections of the population and make schools, colleges, and universities, alongside other parts of formal and informal education within the UK, important sites of population governance. To illustrate this, the chapter will cover how particular knowledge and logics around terrorism, radicalisation, vulnerability, and resilience have created the conditions of possibility within which Prevent has been operationalised as part of a broader *dispositif* of precautionary risk (Aradau and van Munster 2007: 103) to manage students, co-opt practitioners, delimit permissible and non-permissible expression, and minimise risk.

However, before covering this, and to allow for a proper explanation of these issues, the chapter will begin with an overview of Michel Foucault's 'third modality of power'—governmentality—and identify the significant ways in which it differs from his other modalities as well as more traditional theories of power. Power is a concept of central importance across the social sciences, and it is far beyond the scope of this chapter to engage in an in-depth theorisation of it. However, governmentality refers to something specific, the 'conduct of conduct', a form of power that operates 'either directly through large scale campaigns, or indirectly through techniques that will make possible, without the full awareness of the people' (Foucault 1991: 100), the structuring of 'the field of possible action, to act on our own or others' capacities for action' (Dean 1999: 14). To better understand Prevent as a governmental strategy within education, it is necessary first to briefly reflect on power and the ways in which it operates.

## Governmentality and Prevent

In his seminal study on power, Stephen Lukes (2005) distinguishes between three 'views' of power, each of which I will consider briefly below. The first view represents the most straightforward account and approaches the concept as something 'negative' that dominates and restricts and that functions in a linear fashion between different but clearly defined actors. Robert Dahl's theory of power where power is understood as the capacity to which A can get B to do something that B would otherwise not do is a notable and seminal example of such an approach (Dahl 1957: 202–203). Lukes cites Bachrach and Baratz (1970) to discuss the second view of power, which reveals not only the power relations that exist when A makes decisions that directly affect B but also the ability for A to direct their energy into limiting the scope of B's actions to those that either correspond with A's or are 'comparatively innocuous to A' (p. 7). The final and most complex view Lukes speaks of is the third view, which critiques the behavioural focus of the first and second and hones in on the ability to control the political agenda (not necessarily via a formal decisions) and manage a population's 'perceptions, cognitions and preferences in such a way that they accept their role in the existing order of things' (Lukes 2005: 28).

Each of these different views gives some idea of the variance that exists around theorisations of power. Pigeonholing Foucault's theory of power (and its various modalities) into any one of these three would prove difficult, but serves at the very least to demonstrate the radical position he adopts where the concept is understood not as something that exclusively conceals, represses, or censors but is instead *productive*—it 'produces reality; it produces domains of objects and rituals of truth' (Foucault 1977: 194). A particularly significant product of power is knowledge; in fact, knowledge is *always* the product of power and power always the function of knowledge—hence, Foucault's tendency to refer to the joint concept *power/knowledge*. As a consequence of this relationship, multiple different forms of knowledge are 'manufactured and circulated by an institutional matrix, involving the state, politicians, security experts and the media' (Mythen and Walklate 2005: 389).

The production of multiple different forms of knowledge is a very important consideration for the chapter's subsequent sections, and the multiplicity of knowledges produced here alludes to another way in which orthodox theories of power are contradicted by Foucault's model. Power is said to operate via 'capillary functioning' across society (Foucault 1977: 198), and rather than emanating from a centralised location in a direct and linear fashion, it instead 'circulates throughout the entire social body' (Fraser 1981: 278) to constitute agents rather being something that they instrumentally deploy (Gaventa 2003: 1). Significant and serious consequences follow if one adheres to this theory of power, one of which being that power stops being something that can be wholly and precisely wielded and instead is better thought of as a 'machine in which everyone is caught' and never something 'wholly in the hands of one person' (Foucault 1980a: 156). The capillary action that characterises the operation of power within society reveals a more complex and apparently chaotic process; however, it is not without *any* structure, logic, or focal points, and the different forms of power offered by Foucault help to explain this (Foucault 2001: 1391).

Foucault talks of three specific modalities of power: sovereign, disciplinary, and governmental. Sovereign power is *prohibitive*, operating within territories and saying to actors "Don't do this, don't do that" (Foucault 2007: 11). This modality works by 'laying down a law and fixing a punishment for the person who breaks it' (Foucault 2007: 5). Disciplinary power is *prescriptive* and operates through a series of techniques 'which fall within the domain of surveillance, diagnosis, and the possible transformation of individuals' (Foucault 2007: 5). Finally, there is the 'pre-eminent form of power', that of government (Foucault 2007: 108). The art of government or *governmentality* has the population as its target and seeks to manage the entire population via 'an ensemble formed by institutions, procedures, analyses and reflections, calculations, and tactics' (Foucault 2007: 108). Governmentality looks to manage 'things'; it is tasked with managing a whole nexus of interactions between people and their relationships to a vast array of different phenomenon (Foucault 2007: 96). The remit of governmental power, therefore, is far broader than the other aforementioned modalities, but rather than having rule or control as its function (Foucault 2007: 116), it instead represents a form of *management* upon the 'conduct of life' (Dean 1996: 224). Via governmentality we witness the receding of rules and in its place a multiplicity of tactics designed to allow for said management (Foucault 2007: 99).

The complexity is immediately apparent when one considers the management of a domain fraught with an array of relations and interactions and their corresponding variables and uncertainties. Government is tasked with managing 'a space in which a series of uncertain elements unfold… [it must] …plan a milieu in terms of events or series of events of possible elements, of series that will have to be regulated within a multivalent and transformable framework' (Foucault 2007: 20). Management of the milieu requires different techniques and apparatus to other modalities as it seeks to achieve different ends. Seeking circulation (Foucault 2007: 21) as opposed to fixing or imposing, to manage the milieu is to 'let things happen' (Foucault 2007: 45) rather than seeking direct control of every aspect. Governmentality involves accepting and allowing that which is risky, harmful, or inconvenient but seeking to minimise these aspects through the production of governable subjects (Foucault 1991). The salience of governmentality and its value in gaining a wider appreciation of the operation of power has seen it applied to a range of topics as diverse as Japanese public health (Borovoy 2017), big data (Flyverborn et al. 2017), and, of course, terrorism (Barmaki 2014).

Nearly two decades have passed since the events of September 11, yet terrorism remains widely held as the single greatest threat to international security. The securitisation of terrorism provides the common sense rationale for the existence of the Prevent Strategy, but the threat of terrorism alone does not explain the manner in which Prevent and the Prevent Duty operate as means of producing subjects and governing the population. To get a better understanding of how this has been achieved one must investigate the voluminous, complex, and mutually reinforcing series of expert knowledges that have come to prominence as a result of this 'exceptional' and 'unprecedented' threat as well as the routines and practices that they allow and legitimise. In the production and reproduction of these knowledges, 'self-evident truths' concerning the radicalisation process, the vulnerability of individuals, and the need for a resilient population form into discursive regimes with the ability to specify and delimit objects and direct behaviour (Allen 2004: 374). The subtlety of this modality of power means that what appears normal, natural, or even scientific conceals a political project (Gamson et al. 1992: 374) with the governance of the population as its objective.

Prevent and, in particular, the Prevent Duty represent one of the contemporary ways in which the threat and spectre of terrorism has allowed for state responses that have essentially seen the complete reorganisation of 'everyday "normal" political and bureaucratic rationalities' (Mavelii 2013: 161), in this instance refocusing aspects of education towards a counter-terrorism function. As designated 'specified authorities', childcare providers as well as institutions within primary, secondary, further and higher education find themselves having to have 'due regard to the need to prevent people from being drawn into terrorism' (HM Government 2015: 5). At first glance, this may seem like a fairly innocuous statement or perhaps even a positive, progressive, and common sense prescription. However, viewed in a more critical light, it provides the latest piece of evidence for the manner in which national security and civil society have increasingly forged alignments as a means of countering radicalisation (De Goede and Simon 2013: 325), the consequences of which entail the co-option of public sector workers within education and the monitoring and management of students.

The introduction of this statutory duty and its enactment across education have culminated in a variety of policies and practices across the sector to ensure compliance with the law. Through the deployment of this legal framework and connected processes, such as the Channel programme, one sees instances of sovereign and disciplinary power, but more significantly the manifestation of governmental impetus and a 'desire to transform how millions of public sector workers see and engage with their environments' (Martin 2018: 267). As mentioned earlier, this transformation has not been achieved in a direct 'top down' prescriptive fashion, but there are noteworthy and observable focal points from which a 'bottom up' process has emanated. Specific programmes of education for students that focus on teaching 'British Values' (Department for Education 2014) and mandatory training for staff designed to retool them to be more effective at spotting vulnerable students and the behaviours that may indicate they are 'at risk' of radicalisation are two examples of this (HM Government 2016). Such initiatives have successfully cultivated an environment of suspicion and informed practices of surveillance and categorisation (see Chap. 4) in which educators and students serve as both objects and instruments in the 'governmental necessity' (Farrell and Lander 2018: 4) that 'seeks to discipline, train, absorb and neutralise difference within a discourse of shared civic values' (Farrell 2016: 294).

The formal expansion of UK counter-terrorism into education therefore is a contemporary example of what Rogers has previously commented is a 'significant shift in the emphasis of embedding capabilities, and the focus of security-related strategic policy to underpin an emergent governmentality, that seeks to realign ideological thinking and thus citizens' conduct across the breadth of activities that are being generated' (Rogers 2008: 53). Achieving this has required the production of 'a more-or-less cohesive project of risk knowledge which [was] deployed to render terrorism pre-emptively governable' (Heath-Kelly 2013: 395). The remainder of this chapter explores some of the focal points of this risk knowledge and explains how particularly logics around radicalisation, resilience, and vulnerability have been situated within a broader dispositif[1] of 'precautionary risk' (Aradau and van Munster 2007: 103) to co-opt educators into UK counter-terrorism as part of the management of the potential risk posed by vulnerable students.

## The Logics of the Risk Knowledge

The aforementioned practices and processes, explored in greater detail elsewhere in this book, should be understood as the products of salient embedded expert knowledge that produces the conditions of possibility for particular interventions and behaviours and more specifically provides 'civil society workers knowledge frames for signalling polarisation and radicalisation, and toolkits for possible interventions that can be made in cases of concern' (De Goede and Simon 2013: 326). Here, expertise plays 'an extremely important role in modulating social and political practice' (Huysmans 2006: 9) and demonstrates the ability to reduce the complex and unknown into that which is simple and known—even scientific (Mitchell 2002: 15).

Radicalisation, which is defined in the Government's Prevent Duty Guidance as 'the process by which a person comes to support terrorism and extremist ideologies associated with terrorist groups' (2015: 36), is probably the most significant example of a knowledge elevated to the status of truth that legitimises and gives form to strategies of precautionary risk and the governance of subjects within education under the auspice of counter-terrorism. The confidence and frequency with which radicalisation is operationalised within contemporary counter-terrorism strategy imply it is a process of which little ambiguity exists. However, scratch beneath the surface and there does not appear to be a, 'consistent notion of what is meant by "radicalization"' (Richards, 2011: 143).

Chapter 2 covered some of the contestation and disagreement around radicalisation as well as highlighted prominent models of the process; however, what is particularly noteworthy with each of these is the focus

[1] Foucault speaks of a dispositif as 'a thoroughly heterogeneous ensemble consisting of discourses, institutions, architectural forms, regulatory decisions, laws, administrative measures, scientific statements, philosophical, moral and philanthropic propositions – in short, the said as much as the unsaid. Such are the elements of the apparatus. The apparatus itself is the system of relations that can be established between these elements' (Foucault 1980b: 194).

they place on the individual's vulnerability (Blackwood et al. 2016). The absence of certainty over the functioning of a radicalisation process (Taylor and Soni 2017: 248) has allowed for a 'discernible shift away from the examination of the political context of acts of terrorism towards a search for social and psychological factors' (Coppock and McGovern 2014: 246). One key consequence of this is that causes are reframed in the context of the individual and 'indicators' and 'vulnerabilities' become the signifiers of an individual's situation along their radicalisation pathway. The shift in emphasis to identifiable vulnerabilities is the precursor to formalising and collating these which we see in the form of the government's 22 vulnerability indicators (HM Government 2012: 2–3).

The radicalisation discourse lacks explanatory power and in its place offers up a dubious predictive power (Kundnani 2012: 10) premised on a seemingly very broad and ambiguous series of factors. Ethical questions abound as to why counter-terrorism has encroached further and further into different facets of civil society and led to the securitisation of education as well as the other specified authorities. The elevation of a pseudo-scientific radicalisation knowledge to function as the foundational logic upon which the Prevent Strategy and other counter-terrorism interventions are built conceals its constitutive power, that is, the manner in which it 'actually produces (discursively) the threats it claims to identify for the performance of governance, rather than as reacting to the existence of such risks' (Heath-Kelly 2013: 408). A discourse of radicalisation has produced a simplistic linear process that starts with a vulnerable person and ends in violence, thus creating the conditions for the necessity of security interventions, whether this be in the prisons, the hospitals, the classroom, or the lecture theatre.

When radicalisation has been established, the connected discourse of vulnerability to extremism 'is given powerful legitimacy via the development and application of positivistic psychological technologies' (Coppock and McGovern 2014: 250). The 22 vulnerability indicators referenced in Chap. 2 provide one means by which potential risks can be identified and threatened harm made 'knowable, legible and thus actionable' (Martin 2018: 257; Aradau and Van Munster 2008). Radicalisation and the corresponding logic of vulnerability create students as subjects that are both at risk and risky (Heath-Kelly 2012: 83), a duality that is at its sharpest with Muslim children as 'would-be terrorists' (Coppock 2014: 116). Within education, the risks presented by 'vulnerable' young people make actionable interventions upon the individual via various mechanisms of security under the auspice of safeguarding (e.g. Channel referrals) as well as by 'building resilience' through the mandatory study of programmes of education that promote a homogenous set of British Values.

Resilience, a concept taken from ecological sciences and defined by Hardy as 'the capacity of an individual, community or ecosystem to mitigate the impact of a shock or disturbance and then to recover in its aftermath' (Hardy 2015: 82), is a prominent theme within the Prevent Strategy, and alongside safeguarding, it is something schools are expected to help students build 'by fostering a strong ethos and values-based education, as well as by providing a safe space for them to debate controversial issues and develop the critical thinking skills and knowledge they need to be able to challenge extremist arguments' (Educate against Hate 2018). Consequently, citizens (in this instance students) become 'part of the system of preparation for the preservation of the way of life under threat'—a 'governmentality of resilience' that functions within 'at-risk' populations as a means to embed 'practices, ideology [and] ways of thinking' (Rogers 2008: 42) into the citizenry that will mitigate the potential impact of exposure to extremist narratives and the possibility of radicalisation.

In her speech at the Festival of Education in 2017, the Chief Inspector of Ofsted, Amanda Spielman, reiterated the importance of teaching British Values through civic education, describing it as 'critical' (Ofsted 2017). However, as Coppock (2014: 122) highlights, one of the dangers around singling out these values as 'the gold standard' is the manner in which 'Muslim culture, traditions and values are pathologised as "other" and considered a threat to British society'. More broadly, as argued by Hardy, the appropriateness of resilience as an organising principle for counter-terrorism exhibits more fundamental problems insofar as it securitises 'civil relief efforts by raising them to the level of national security' and promotes a 'state of permanent civil anxiety' (Hardy 2015: 83–84; see also Walker and Cooper 2011: 154). Again, a concept drawn from the natural sciences and presenting a seemingly neutral and apolitical position on responding to terror risk renders the public sectors 'de facto extensions of the police and security' (Hardy 2015: 88) services tasked with carrying out a governmental strategy to identify those who may become terrorists and intervening in their lives to build resilience as a 'critical' function of their education.

The discourses of radicalisation, vulnerability, and resilience are examples of those that give form to a dispositif of precautionary risk—an assemblage that encourages hyper-vigilance and one that asks us to 'constantly look over our shoulders and [be] suspicious of the person standing next to us' (Carter 2017: 24). The unknowns of the world and the future as something that has the potential to unleash catastrophic destructive consequences are taken as the intuitive launching pad to try and expose the unintelligibility of these unknowns—in this case the clandestine would-be terrorist. Anticipation, prediction, and intervention are the order of the day in the face of such 'anticipatory epistemic objects' (Anderson 2007), and subsequently security practices and technologies are deployed to anticipate this uncertain future (Amoore 2009), 'ideally occurring before a threat has actually emerged' (Anderson 2010: 790). Put another way, the Prevent Strategy '...exhibits a preoccupation with the future oriented temporality, that is, something could happen in the future, which in conjunction with the immanency of the threat justifies corrective interventions in the present' (Elshimi 2015: 111).

The 'key indicators' of radicalisation (see Chap. 2) and their role in making legible the transition from citizen to terrorist help, we argue, to create alternative subjectivities and sites of intervention. Once legible, the pre-emptive logics of anticipatory security allow for action in the present as a means of tackling that which will occur if allowed to develop undisturbed. We see this with the Prevent Duty and the expansion of counter-terrorism within education. Students are potential risks and are thus subjected to sovereign, disciplinary, and governmental forms of power *in the present* to observe whether they are demonstrating the characteristics of vulnerability and to prevent them from realising their potential as would-be terrorists. The management of this section of the population, especially when considered alongside the other specialised authorities, demonstrates how the production of a risk knowledge and a broader dispositif of precautionary risk has created the conditions of possibility for the governance of whole swathes of the UK citizenry and co-opted people with no background in counter-terrorism to operate as overseers in this process.

## Conclusions

The formal expansion of Prevent into various areas of the public sector has been justified on account of the severity of the threat, the requirement to anticipate the unknown, the vulnerability of citizens to radicalisation, and the need for a whole-of-society approach to counter-terrorism. As Home Secretary Sajid Javid put it in a recent speech:

> There's an ongoing battle. A battle for hearts and minds. It will be won in the schools. It will be won in the mosques. And on our social media. And we must all play our role. (Home Office 2018)

In excerpts such as this one, we see the utterance of what may appear a prudent or even necessary response to terrorism. However, what we have sought to demonstrate here is that while this may increasingly have become the 'new normal' of counter-terrorism, the common sense knowledge that deems it necessary to extend these security practices into education conceals the expansion of broader neoliberal governmentality. As Mythen and Walklate (2005: 391–392) write, 'the governmentality thesis gives voice to the possibility that interest groups are able to use their strategic capabilities to capitalize on unforeseen events…providing the political lexicon through which ulterior motives are being camouflaged'.

The ulterior motive in this instance is the expansion of UK counter-terrorism efforts into areas of civil society where it does not belong and where, rather than simply being in place to respond to this single issue, it represents another aspect of a wider political project that will have grave consequences for education specifically and civil society more broadly. Educators, already stretched and expected to do 'more for less' in times of economic austerity, find themselves taking on further responsibilities for which they are ill-prepared while at the same time students' scope for critical thought and expression will likely be inhibited, especially in the case of ethnic minority and Muslim students where 'racialised optics' are applied (Puwar 2004: 51). For civil society, the ability for education to transform the lives of young people is hindered by the encroachment of the national security agenda into this space, which continues to skew the attention given to terrorism within the UK, amplifies societal anxiety, and undermines the potential that exists for education to provide social mobility at a time, to take one statistic, where rates of child poverty in the UK is increasing (McGuinness 2018: 3).

Terrorism provides the seminal object within the dispostif of precautionary risk, and around it, we have witnessed the formation of productive discourses of radicalisation, vulnerability, and resilience that have tremendous legitimising power to provide the logic around which the Prevent Duty has been deployed in schools, colleges, and universities. As we have demonstrated in this chapter, however, these discourses lack evidence for their own claims and contain a number of intuitive sounding but unsubstantiated assumptions. Despite this, they have successfully been elevated to the status of science or truth and have enabled the unprecedented encroachment of counter-terrorism, mobilising mechanisms of security within education, producing new technologies and practices of surveillance, intervening on those individuals deemed vulnerable and who are progressing down a radicalisation pathway, and promoting an ambiguous and ill-defined set of hegemonic mono-cultural values as part of the mandated education (Ford 2017: 150–151).

Prevent's expansion represents the latest incarnation of a desire to identify 'known unknowns' (see Rumsfeld 2002) and reduce risk at all costs—underlying such response is a sense of what we do not know cannot be tolerated. Positivistic psychology provides 'enormous appeal' in this endeavour and 'appears to offer answers and "certainty" in a world characterised by uncertainty and, on occasion, chaos' (Coppock and McGovern 2014: 248). These pseudo-scientific techniques and tools provide a veneer of objectivity, rationality, and neutrality that purport to allow practitioners within education to conduct their duty without feelings of guilt or the need for extensive training, safe in the knowledge that their limited guidance comes as a result of extensive evidence-based research. The reality is anything but, and the training and toolkit provided only serve to dress up counter-terrorism as an intervention of care.

Through the Prevent Duty, civil society has been further subsumed within the GWoT. A powerful productive risk knowledge has created its own *raison d'être* and brought a raft of governmental policies directly into the lecture theatre and classroom as well as co-opting educators as instruments of this strategy. Particularly worrying is the way in which the Duty has repackaged social and political dissatisfaction and grievance as possible indicators of risk, rendering the tradition of radical thought within HE difficult, particularly for Muslim students (Brown and Saeed 2015). Away from HE, given that one of the government's aims with its mandated citizenship education that is mandated at key stages 3 and 4 is to equip pupils with 'the skills to think critically and debate political questions' (Department of Education 2013: 1), one wonders how they expect the Duty to help achieve this aim.

There has been, and will continue to be, much contestation and disagreement as to what the Duty 'is'. However one views the Duty, what is beyond doubt is that Prevent is one strand of the UK's counter-terrorism strategy, and since 2015, it has been formally deployed across civil society. Within the context of an unknowable future, Prevent has entered UK education and its prescriptions, 'while presented as managerial, technical and pastoral, are deeply political' (Martin 2014: 63). The Prevent Duty provides an explicit, contemporary example of the a neoliberal governmentality that aims to better classify, control, and manage the population and that demonstrates the manner in which the GWoT has extended from the sovereign demonstrations of power in the Middle East to the disciplinary and governmental techniques 'at home'.

## References


Allen, J. 2004. "Power in its institutional guises". In G. Hughes and R. Fergusson (eds,) *Orderly Lives, Family, Work and Welfare*. London: Routledge.

Amoore, L. 2009. "Algorithmic war: Everyday geographies of the war on terror", *Antipode* 41(1): 49–69.

Anderson, B. 2007. "Hope for nanotechnology: Anticipatory knowledge and the governance of affect", *Area*, 39(2):156–165.

Anderson, B. 2010. "Preemption, precaution, preparedness: Anticipatory action and future Geographies", *Progress in Human Geography*, 34(6): 777–798.

Aradau, C. and van Munster, R. 2007. "Governing terrorism through risk: Taking precautions, (un)knowing the future", *European Journal of International Relations*, 13(1): 89–115.

Aradau, C. and Van Munster, R. 2008. "Taming the future: The *dispositif* of risk in the war on terror". In L. Amoore and M. De Goede (eds.) *Risk and the War on Terror*. Abingdon: Routledge: 23–40.

Bachrach, P. and Baraz, M. S. 1970. *Power and Poverty: Theory and Practice*. New York: Oxford University Press.

Barmaki, R. 2014. "Security, life, and death: governmentality and biopower in the post 9/11 ear", *Global Change, Peace & Security*, 26(2): 229–231.

Blackwood, L., Hopkins, N. and Reicher, S. 2016. "From theorizing radicalization to surveillance practices: Muslims in the cross hairs of scrutiny", *Political Psychology*, 37(5): 597–612.

Borovoy, A. 2017. "Japan's public health paradigm: governmentality and the containment of harmful behaviour", *Medical Anthropology: Cross-Cultural Studies in Health and Illness*, 36(1): 32–46.

Brown, K. E. and Saeed, T. 2015. "Radicalisation and counter-radicalisation at British Universities: Muslim encounters and alternatives", *Ethnic Racial Studies*, 38(11): 1952–1698.

Carter, D. M. 2017. "(De)constructing difference: a qualitative review of the 'othering' of UK Muslim communities, extremism, soft harms, and Twitter analytics", *Behavioral Sciences of Terrorism and Political Aggression*, 9(1): 21–36.

Coppock, V. 2014. "'Can you Spot a Terrorist in Your Classroom?' Problematising the Recruitment of Schools to the 'War on Terror' in the United Kingdom", *Global Studies of Childhood*, 4(2): 115–125.

Coppock, V. and McGovern, M. 2014. "'Dangerous Minds'? Deconstructing Counter-Terrorism Discourse, Radicalisation and the 'Psychological Vulnerability' of Muslim Children and Young People in Britain", *Children & Society*, 28(3): 242–256.

Dahl, R. A. 1957. "The concept of Power", *Systems Research and Behavioral Science*, 2(3): 201–215.

Dean, M. 1996. "Foucault, government and the enfolding of authority". In Barry, A., Osbourne, T. & Rose, N. (eds). *Foucault and political reason: Liberalism, neo-liberalism and rationalities of government*. Chicago: Chicago University Press: 209–229.

Dean, M. 1999. *Governmentality: Power and Rule in Modern Society*. Gateshead: SAGE Publications.

De Goede, M. and Simon, S. 2013. "Governing Future Radicals in Europe", *Antipode*, 45(2): 315–335.

Department of Education. 2013. "Citizenship programmes of study: Key stages 3 and 4". Available at: https://assets.publishing.service.gov.uk/government/uploads/system/uploads/attachment_data/file/239060/SECONDARY_national_curriculum_-_Citizenship.pdf.

Department for Education. 2014. "Promoting fundamental British value as part of SMSC in schools". Available at: https://assets.publishing.service.gov.uk/government/uploads/system/uploads/attachment_data/file/380595/SMSC_Guidance_Maintained_Schools.pdf.

Educate against Hate. 2018. "The Prevent Duty". Available at: https://educate-againsthate.com/about/.

Elshimi, M. 2015. "De-radicalisation interventions as technologies of the self: a Foucauldian analysis", *Critical Studies on Terrorism*, 8(1): 110–129.

Farrell, F. 2016. "'Why all of a sudden do we need to teach fundamental British values?' A critical investigation of religious education student teacher positioning within a policy discourse of discipline and control", *Journal of Education for Teaching: International research and pedagogy*, 42(3): 280–297.

Farrell, F. and Lander, V. 2018. "'We're not British values teachers are we?': Muslim teachers' subjectivity and the governmentality of unease", *Educational Review* (early access).

Flyverborn, M., Madsen, A. K. and Rasche, A. 2017. "Big data as governmentality in international development: Digital traces, algorithms, and altered visibilities", *Information Society*, 33(1): 35–42.

Ford, K. 2017. "Developing a peace perspective on counter-extremist education", *Peace Review*, 29(2): 144–152.

Foucault, M. 1977. *Discipline and punish: The birth of the prison*. Translated from French by Alan Sheridan. London: Penguin Books.

Foucault, M. 1980a. "The eye of power". In Colin Gordon (ed.) *Power/Knowledge: Selected interviews and other writings 1972–1977*. Translated from French by

Colin Gordon, Leo Marshall, John Mepham and Kate Soper. London: Harvester Wheatsheaf: 78–108.

Foucault, M. 1980b. "The confessions of the flesh". In Colin Gordon (ed.) *Power/Knowledge: Selected interviews and other writings 1972–1977*. Translated from French by Colin Gordon, Leo Marshall, John Mepham and Kate Soper. London: Harvester Wheatsheaf: 194–228.

Foucault, M. 1991. "On Governmentality", *Ideology and Consciousness*, 6: 5–21.

Foucault, M. 2001. *Dits et ecrits I, 1954–1975*. Paris: Quatro Gallimard.

Foucault, M. 2007. In Michel Senellart (ed.) *Security, Territory, Population: Lectures at the College de France 1977-1978*. Translated from French by Graham Burchell. Basingstoke: Palgrave Macmillan.

Fraser, N. 1981. "Foucault on modern power: Empirical insights and normative confusions", *Praxis International*, 3(1): 272–287.

Gamson, W. A., Croteau, D., Hoynes, W., & Sasson, T. 1992. "Media images and the social construction of reality", *Annual review of sociology*, 18: 373–393.

Gaventa, J. 2003. *Power after Lukes: a review of the literature*. Brighton: Institute of Development Studies.

Hardy, K. 2015. "Resilience in UK counter-terrorism", *Theoretical Criminology*, 19(1): 77–94.

Heath-Kelly, C. 2012. "Reinventing prevention or exposing the gap? False positives in UK terrorism governance and the quest for pre-emption", *Critical Studies on Terrorism*, 5(1): 69–87.

Heath-Kelly, C. 2013. "Counter-Terrorism and the Counterfactual: Producing the 'Radicalisation' discourse and the UK Prevent Strategy", *The British Journal of Politics and International Relations*, 15(3): 394–415.

HM Government. 2012. "Channel: Vulnerability assessment framework". Available at: https://assets.publishing.service.gov.uk/government/uploads/system/uploads/attachment_data/file/118187/vul-assessment.pdf

HM Government. 2015. "Prevent duty guidance". Available at: https://www.legislation.gov.uk/ukdsi/2015/9780111133309/pdfs/ukdsiod_9780111133309_en.pdf

HM Government. 2016. "Prevent: Training Catalogue". Available at: https://educateagainsthate.com/wp-content/uploads/2018/01/Prevent_Training_catalogue_-_March_2016.pdf

Home Office. 2018. "Home Secretary announces new counter-terrorism strategy". Available at: https://www.gov.uk/government/speeches/home-secretary-announces-new-counter-terrorism-strategy

Huysmans, J. 2006. *The politics of insecurity: Fear, migrations and asylum in the EU*. Abingdon: Routledge.

Kundnani, A. 2012. "Radicalisation: the journey of a concept", *Race and Class*, 54(2): 3–25.

Lukes, S. 2005. *Power: A Radical View*. London: Palgrave Macmillan.

Martin, T. 2014. "Governing an unknowable future: the politics of Britain's Prevent Policy", *Critical Studies on Terrorism*, 7(1): 62–78.

Martin, T. 2018. "Identifying potential terrorists: Visuality, security and the Chanel project", *Security Dialogue*, 49(4): 254–271.

Mavelli, L. 2013. "Between normalisation and exception: The securitisation of Islam and the construction of the secular subject", *Millennium: Journal of International Studies*, 41(2): 159–181.

McGuinness, F. 2018. "Poverty in the UK: statistics, house of Commons Library". Available at: https://researchbriefings.parliament.uk/ResearchBriefing/Summary/SN07096#fullreport

Mitchell, T. 2002. *Rule of Experts*. Berkeley: University of California Press.

Mythen, G. and Walklate, M. 2005. "Criminology and terrorism: Which thesis? Risk society or governmentality?", *The British Journal of Criminology*, 46(3): 379–398.

Ofsted. 2017. "Amanda Spielman's speech at the Festival of Education". Available at: https://www.gov.uk/government/speeches/amanda-spielmans-speech-at-the-festival-of-education

Puwar, N. 2004. *Space invaders: Race, gender and bodies out of place*. Berg: King's Lynn.

Richards, A. 2011. "The problem with "radicalization": The remit of "Prevent" and the need to refocus on terrorism in the UK", *International Affairs*, 87(1): 143–152.

Rogers, P. 2008. "Contesting and Preventing Terrorism: On the Development of UK Strategic Policy on Radicalisation and Community Resilience", *Journal of Policing, Intelligence and Counter Terrorism*, 3(2): 38–61.

Rumsfeld, D. 2002. "Press Conference by U.S. Secretary of Defence, Donald Rumsfeld". Available at: https://www.nato.int/docu/speech/2002/s020606g.htm

Taylor, L. and Soni, A. 2017. "Preventing radicalisation: a systematic review of literature considering the lived experience of the UK's Prevent strategy in educational settings", *Pastoral Care in Education*, 35(4): 241–252.

Walker, J. and Cooper, M. 2011. "Genealogies of resilience: From systems adaptation to the political economy of crisis adaptation", *Security Dialogue*, 42(2): 143–160.

CHAPTER 6

# Education and (Counter-)Terrorism

**Abstract** This chapter provides an international overview of some of the different ways in which education has been utilised as a means to prevent or reduce violence. The chapter begins by providing the conventional wisdom that is offered to explain why young people are particularly susceptible to radicalisation and the value education is said to have in preventing or disrupting this process as well as building student resilience. The chapter then explores a range of educational initiatives designed to reduce violence, focusing primarily on dedicated programmes but also covering peace education, citizenship education, and the broader ways in which counter-radicalisation strategies have sought to draw on the education sector. The chapter concludes by acknowledging the positive contribution that education can have in the production of peace and the promotion of non-violence, but argues that the manner and context within which this is achieved are very important and that clumsy efforts to teach particular values or a version of citizenship as a means of countering terrorism endanger securitising education, removing the scope for critical thought and alienating and stigmatising specific students and student populations.

**Keywords** Countering Violent Extremism (CVE) • Education • Peace



I. Awan et al., *Terrorism in the Classroom*, Palgrave Studies in Risk, Crime and Society,
https://doi.org/10.1007/978-3-030-01710-1_6

## Introduction

In the wake of the Global War on Terror, the severity and seriousness of terrorism have seen it become the major focus of national security strategies across the globe, including in the UK, where it has been categorised as a 'tier one' security threat (HM Government 2015: 87). However, those governments that assess the threat from terrorism as severe do not approach the phenomenon as an isolated and spontaneous event but as the result of a process of 'radicalisation' that culminates in violence (see Chaps. 2 and 5). The perpetrators of this form of political violence are said to travel down a pathway or undergo a process in which grievances or perceptions of injustice are intensified until they galvanise into concrete 'us and them thinking' and a willingness to use violence as a means of addressing or righting perceived wrongs. Approaching an individual's decision to carry out terroristic violence as the culmination of a linear (but not uniform) process presents the governments tasked with reducing and preventing terrorism with an opportunity to intervene and disrupt in the period of time 'before the bomb goes off' (Neumann 2008: 4). Such interventions have taken many forms, but education is one sector in which such interpositions are considered particularly important because of the perceived vulnerability of young people and the ability to engage with them *en masse*.[1]

Education's capacity to counter extremism, disrupt radicalisation, and build resilience will be the focus of this chapter, and herein we will focus on contemporary knowledge pertaining to countering violent extremism (CVE), promoting non-violence, building resilience, and so forth within education as well as exploring a range of international counter-extremism strategies to identify how they incorporate education. The chapter's predominant contribution will be to provide an international overview of a series of specific, tailored CVE programmes, educational initiatives that are included within a broader CVE strategy, as well as other closely related programmes designed to achieve similar objectives. The chapter will conclude by considering the criticisms levelled at the expansion of the security

[1] Taking the UK as an example, in January 2018 there were 8.74 million pupils in primary and secondary education (Department of Education 2018) and 2.32 million in HE (UK Universities 2018).

agenda into education and reflect on what role education can play in creating engaged citizens, reducing violence, and promoting peace.

## Young People, Radicalisation, and Building Resilience Through Education

Young people are considered to be particularly vulnerable to radicalisation via extremist ideologies, as 'they seek to uncover their own identity, look to bolster self-confidence and are in search of meaning in their lives' (Ghosh et al. 2017: 119). When considering Islamist terrorism (as much of the literature does), the way in which this occurs tends to be characterised in popular public discourse as happening either via a 'radical religious leader' operating within an orthodox religious community or as a result of 'self-radicalisation' via exposure to extremist material online (Hayes 2017: 153). This is a dichotomy that we see reproduced in the strategic context section of the latest iteration of the UK's counter-terrorism strategy CONTEST and the website *Educate Against Hate*, an online resource developed by the Department for Education and the Home Office:

> Daesh and Al Qa'ida exploit the internet to promote warped alternative narratives... [and]...cynically groom the vulnerable and the young to join their movement, inspiring people within our own communities to commit senseless acts of violence. (HM Government 2018: 7)

> Anyone can be vulnerable to extremism and radicalisation, but children are particularly at risk. As they grow and become more independent, it is not unusual for them to take risks, explore new things and push boundaries. Teenage years are often a time when young people will be searching for answers to questions about identity, faith and belonging, as well as looking for adventure and excitement. Extremist groups know young people are vulnerable and may claim to offer them answers, identity and a strong social network, and using the internet and social media to spread their ideology. (Educate Against Hate 2018)

Given the extent to which young people are said to be vulnerable, education is viewed as having a double value: first, as a space in which young people can be engaged/observed and, second, as a means to teach, instil, and challenge. Focusing on the latter, the importance of education 'cannot be understated' (Moffett and Sgro 2016: 145) due to its proactive and preventative position in what is commonly perceived to be a broadly linear process of radicalisation (Ghosh et al. 2017: 120), its ability to serve as 'early warning' to detect extremism (Subedi 2017), and more positively its ability to foster ethical behaviour, build resilience, develop students' ability to think critically, and maintain open-mindedness (Ghosh et al. 2017: 120; Bensalah Alaoui 2017: 112). Consequently, schools, childcare providers, colleges, and universities provide convenient spaces where swathes of young people can be targeted as part of specific programmes of education that seek to achieve these objectives, which often come under the heading of CVE.

As the above text alludes to, despite some consensus around the necessity of education as a sector and means with which radicalisation can be prevented and disrupted, knowledge concerning how best to utilise this space and conduct CVE here demonstrates a higher degree of heterogeneity. Not only do different initiatives operate with different theories of change that link content, activities, and assumptions to the desired objective (Herrington 2015: 30), but what works and what is likely to work in particular locales is contested, in part, because the ability for education to effectively build resilience is 'highly complex' and requires consideration of 'cultural, social, and religious aspects of the societies in which programmes are to take place thus avoiding over-generalizations' (Taylor et al. 2017: 196).

Consequently, the use of education to counter violent extremism looks very different around the globe, and complicating things further is the fact that education is often used to achieve similar or overlapping objectives to CVE without necessarily using this terminology. CVE, which is defined by Zeiger and Aly (2015: 2) as programs and policies for countering and preventing radicalisation and recruitment into violent extremism and terrorism as part of an overall counter-terrorism strategy and framework', can and *does* cover an array of diverse initiatives but should not be considered a catch-all term for all methods employed with the objective of promoting non-violence. To provide one example of what we mean here, peace education (Harris 2004) pre-dates the contemporary focus on CVE but is a direct influencer on many modern CVE educational projects and is designed to teach attitudes, values, and skills that will bring about 'behaviour changes that will enable children, youth and adults to prevent conflict and violence, both overt and structural; to resolve conflict peacefully; and to create the conditions conducive to peace' (Fountain 1999: i).

To speak of counter-terrorism/counter-radicalisation/counter-extremism within the education sector therefore is to speak of two different but often coinciding approaches: first, programmes of education integrated into curriculums and, second, the formal co-option of educators to conduct a mandated counter-terrorism function. While these programmes of education have not been without controversy of their own on accounts of their content and delivery, what is typically considered to be the most controversial way in which the education sector and counter-terrorism have come together is in the extension of disciplinary and governmental practices (see Chap. 5) characterised by the monitoring and surveillance of students by their educators (see Chaps. 4 and 7). As the latter has been the focus of several chapters in this book, what is included in this chapter is an analysis of some of the knowledge around education's role in countering extremism, building resilience, and promoting peace, and a review of the international landscape of educational initiatives designed to achieve these objectives.

## Education and CVE in the International Context

Due to the centrality that is placed on the violent ideologies that underpin terrorism and their ability to act as mobilising factors in the process of radicalisation, one particular theory of change links the promotion of alternative values, good citizenship, and rights and responsibilities to challenge these ideologies at their core. UNICEF's Rights Respecting Schools Award represents one of the furthest reaching programmes of rights education, with over 4800 schools currently involved with the programme that puts the UN Convention on the Rights of the Child at the heart of schools in the UK (UNICEF 2018). Davies (2018: 28) synthesises some of the limited research that currently exists around the success of this programme and paints a broadly positive picture of its results in the classroom, with parents, and across the local communities.

More explicitly linked to the counter-terrorism agenda, the UK's Prevent Strategy has recently placed a significant focus on educating young people about the 'British Values' of democracy, the rule of law, individual liberty, and mutual respect for and tolerance of those with different faiths and beliefs and for those without faith. By promoting these specific values the government hopes to achieve one of the core objectives of 'challenging the ideology that supports terrorism and those who promote it' (HM Government 2011: 43). Consequently, schools are required to promote these in the classroom as part of a broader citizenship education that now makes up a statutory national curriculum subject for key stages 3 and 4 (Department of Education 2013). Similar approaches have been adopted in other European countries, and in 2015, France launched the *Grande mobilisation de l'Ecole pour les values de la Republique* (Ministere de l'Education Nationale 2015) with the aim of combating radicalisation among young people by promotion of egalitarian values and citizenship (Ghosh et al. 2016: 44). That we see similarities such as this between the UK and its neighbours in Europe should not come as a surprise as Prevent is considered to be the 'pioneer' in this field, and despite the government's approach having divided opinion, it has been a model that European countries in particular have sought to emulate to varying degrees (Vidino and Brandon 2012: 164).

Germany, Sweden, and Denmark all place an onus on a similar citizenship education approach that pays particular attention to tolerance and democracy. The German counter-extremism strategy includes promoting democracy in its title, and the first stated action area is 'political education, intercultural learning and democracy work'. Strengthening democratic awareness and accepting social diversity are identified as key issues promoted both formally through the taught curriculum and often through institutions subsidised via agencies such as the Federal Agency for Civic Education and the Federal Child and Youth Plan to provide alternative means of political education, for example, in the form of inter-school competitions, local journalist programmes, and trips to Israel (German Federal Government 2016: 17). Promoting democracy and establishing respect for human rights make up part of a compulsory school curriculum in Sweden (Government Offices of Sweden 2011: 26), while in neighbouring Denmark, primary and secondary education have placed 'a greater focus on strengthening pupils' critical faculties and democratic skill' by making human rights a fixed part of the national curriculum (Danish Ministry of Immigration Integration and Housing 2016: 21). Of course, these programmes are not reflective of the respective nations' entire strategies, and projects more explicitly focusing on extremism (both far-right and Islamist) and that are designed to operate at different stages of the radicalisation are also in place and in some cases have been in place for some time (Davies 2018: 16–19).

The Netherlands Counterterrorism Strategy is one where you get a clear sense of just how influential the UK's CONTEST strategy has been (National Coordinator for Security and Counterterrorism 2016). This strategy is broken down into a familiar-sounding series of 'Ps': Procure, Prevent, Protect, Prepare, and Pursue, and within the section on Prevent the strategy stresses the need to identify and tackle radicalisation early, requiring 'working closely with other sectors in a multidisciplinary approach' that includes education (National Coordinator for Security and Counterterrorism 2016: 13). Their 2007–2011 Polarisation and Radicalisation Action Plan (Dutch Ministry of the Interior and Kingdom Relations 2007) provides one of the clearest insights into how the Dutch government views radicalisation, intends to prevent it, and clarifies the role of education as part of this strategy. Citizenship and social integration are identified as the 'core goal in education' (Dutch Ministry of the Interior and Kingdom Relations 2007: 17), and given that the Netherlands approach radicalisation as primarily a sociopolitical issue rather than a religious one, their strategy aims to tackle issues of isolation and polarisation and 'enhance social cohesion by facilitating the integration of alienated groups into mainstream society' (Rabasa et al. 2010: 141). This means efforts to prevent radicalisation have national and local implications, and consequently educators are expected to perform prevention, signalling, and intervention functions, including promoting discussions about various ideologies, monitoring school drop-outs (on the 'soft' side), and enforcing compulsory school attendance and rules of conduct (on the 'hard' side) (Dutch Ministry of the Interior and Kingdom Relations: 11–12).

Education that promotes particular values and encourages good citizenship goes beyond these European examples, and while India does not have a specific CVE programme that runs within the education sector, it does indirectly promote particular values as part of courses on morality, civics, citizenship, and human rights (Ghosh et al. 2016: 40). Meanwhile, neighbouring Bangladesh makes it a requirement that particular 'moral and spiritual values' are taught as part of the national curriculum, including 'justice, a sense of duty, discipline and etiquette, non-communalism, human rights, accommodative attitudes toward corporate living, curiosity, friendliness and perseverance' (Ghosh et al. 2016: 40–41).

These examples draw upon a pre-existing knowledge around citizenship education to enable students to understand their rights and responsibilities as individuals and within broader society. In a similar fashion, peace education represents another influence upon the design of CVE programmes with the intention of integrating peacebuilding into the pedagogical approach to produce change by giving young people enhanced capacity to avoid and deescalate conflict. Cook, citing programmes of education devised by peace societies in the twentieth century, identifies four aspects at the heart of peace education's pedagogy: values clarification and analysis, critical thinking, the development of an ethic of caring, and conflict management and resolution skills (Cook 2008: 894). Many of these aspects are seen duplicated by Ghosh et al. (2017: 119), who, writing in the Canadian context, argue that the Canadian government's counter-terrorism strategy is too reactive, too focused on the terrorist attack rather than pre-empting such an attack and looking to interject in the process of radicalisation via education. Consequently, they recommend that any good education that can effectively counter violent religious extremism should promote values of citizenship and diversity, ensuring a critical approach that can develop 'an understanding of history and power relations in society' and develop religious and media literacy (Ghosh et al. 2017: 127).

Similar principles and recommendations have been put into practice as part of a number of initiatives across the globe. For example, the *Education for Peace* integrative curriculum in Bosnia and Herzegovina (Danesh 2008) has sought to develop critical thinking, emotional insight, creative experience, and constructive action amongst students to help those affected by the 1992–1995 civil war and allow them to better apply the principles of peace to their 'personal, interpersonal, familial and community lives' (Danesh 2008: 164–165). In Australia, the *Beyond Bali* package was designed to develop community resilience in the aftermath of the Bali bombings of 2002 and 2005, events identified as a 'coming of age' for Australia and ones that directly confronted Australia and its neighbours for the first time (Taylor et al. 2017: 194). Consequently, *Beyond Bali*, a transformative learning curriculum package, was designed to provide 'a global perspective and provide opportunities to develop knowledge skills and values about the places and societies people live in, people's capacity to choose and shape preferred futures, peace building, collaborative action and shared responsibility, critical thinking, and responsible values and attitudes' (Taylor et al. 2017: 198). Peacebuilding initiatives have also been identified in over 100 civil society networks throughout Pakistan, which included schools (Mirahmadi et al. 2012: 11).

The indicative content of such programmes is one aspect of what is deemed to contribute towards their success or failure, but so too is their deployment and the availability of appropriate support and interpersonal relationships within and outside formal education. The role a wider network of people, communities, and institutions can play in CVE touches on research and practice that goes beyond this chapter's exclusive focus on education, nevertheless, the placement of educational institutions within such networks provides further useful insight. In the Russian context, for example, Gorbunova highlights the importance of complimenting the efforts of educational institutions to reject extremist ideologies alongside the involvement of young people in positive social activities that integrate their peers and adults as a means of providing the space for open discussion (Gorbunova 2016: 2–3). Subedi identifies the *Living Together Safer* and *Building Community Grants Program* as two Australian initiatives that demonstrate the importance broader community partnerships (of which educational institutions make up part) serve to promote a soft-security approach that will better achieve social integration and a more effective means of countering home-grown extremism through the formation of an early warning system premised on local reliable information (Subedi 2017: 136–138).

When effective adult-child relationships can be formed and youth are supported within their communities and families as well as their schools, then they are more likely to have the 'necessary protective factors in place to counteract the negative, hateful messages purported by violent extremism' (Hayes 2017: 158). The importance of pastoral support and adult-child relationships for effective conflict resilience is well evidenced in the work of groups like International Alert alongside what Syrian and Lebanese community-based groups have been doing with young Syrians directly affected by the ongoing civil war. Children who are experiencing, 'strong feeling of guilt and shame, and a heavy burden of responsibility' as well as anger and a desire for revenge, have been able to effectively share their fears and concerns via, 'supportive social networks, role models, and mentors, accompanied by the creation of physical and emotional safe spaces' (Brooks 2017: 170–172). Fostering meaningful relationships and providing the requisite support for young people meant that they were more likely to disclose and try to work through situations that were troubling them, 'including cases of abuse and exploitation, or attempted recruitment by armed groups', and giving up of weapons they previously carried to feel safe (Brooks 2017: 172).

The increase in research investigating conflict through a gendered lens in recent decades (Enloe 1990; Tickner 2001) has brought to the fore both women's role as perpetrators and facilitators of political violence (Sjoberg and Gentry 2007) and their essential role in peacebuilding (Hudson 2009; Hunt 2002; Lindborg 2017; Davies 2008). This knowledge has informed a number of specific initiatives as well as efforts to try and promote women's involvement in peacebuilding (Ellerby 2013; Goetz and Jenkins 2016), but should be considered alongside warnings that CVE efforts that put an onus on women's roles have often instrumentalised women (Giscard d'Estaing 2017).

We can see examples of specific women's networks such as the UK-based *Women Against Radicalisation* (2018) and the *Muslim Women's Network* (2018) that provide a clear educational function albeit with differing extents to which counter-radicalisation is a primary function. Outside of the UK, particular governments have integrated women into particular efforts to counter violent extremism, and in Morocco, for instance, the state-governed Mursheeda programme is notable for its training of 'female religious leaders and scholars' in 'psychology, law, history, communication and religion' so that they can work within communities and public institutions (Ghosh et al. 2016: 38–39). Efforts have also been made here to promote a 'true image' of peaceful Islam that is 'women friendly' (Bensalah Alaoui 2017: 110).

De Leede et al. (2017: 35–38) provide numerous international examples of CVE good practice that work with women specifically, including The Women Without Borders, *Mothers' Schools* project that was launched in 2008 and aims to support and enhance mothers' agency skills in part so they can better safeguard their families against radicalisation (De Leede et al. 2017: 36) but moreover to focus on capacity building, gender-based violence, female leadership, and intercultural dialogue (Women Without Borders 2018). As of 2018, their website claims to have engaged over 'two thousand mothers in twelve countries across Western and Eastern Europe, south and Southeast Asia, the Middle East, and Sub-Saharan Africa' (Women Without Borders 2018).

Given the predominant focus that is placed on Islamic extremism as the most significant ideology that contributes towards the process of radicalisation, religious education has been another area of specific focus which has informed particular CVE strategies and programmes. The form this takes differs quite considerably internationally; for example, certain schools in the UK have utilised religious education classes as a forum to discuss extremism and inter-faith tension (Davies 2018), while more cohesive approaches such as the *Ethics and Religious Culture* programme in Canada have sought to indirectly counter violent extremism by increasing religious literacy via an exploration of Québec's religious heritage and 'the elements of other religious traditions more recently found in Québec society' (Ministère de l'Éducation et de l'Enseignement supérieur 2018).

Of course, these softer approaches are contrasted quite significantly by the more proscriptive way in which certain nations have had to reform their approach to teaching religion as a result of the GWOT. For example, the former USA President Bush's *Muslim Education Initiative* that was funded by USAID and deployed in Tanzania to produce teaching material, train teachers, and produce a new curriculum of religious education was singled out by critics as essentially being a very thinly veiled move to producing and teaching a version of Islam more in keeping with US interests (Tamim and Smith 2010: 123). While not a party to the GWOT, China is another notable example of a nation that has imposed tight centralised control of religion and is 'increasingly using centralised religious education for CVE goals' (Ghosh et al. 2016: 40–41).

While the West has seen CVE and education as a site of 'surveillance and psycho-social intervention', those nations at the heart of the GWOT such as Iraq, Afghanistan, and Pakistan have seen similar initiatives linked much more explicitly to US/UK counter-insurgency strategy, 'with funding and school construction used as a mechanism for winning hearts and minds' (Novelli 2017: 847). Sitting alongside the broader development goals of halving Middle Eastern literacy and bridging the digital divide, the 9/11 Commission is clear when it states 'education that teaches tolerance, the dignity and value of each individual, and respect for different beliefs is a key element in any global strategy to eliminate Islamist terrorism' before recommending international efforts to contribute funds to build and operate primary and secondary schools in 'those Muslim states that commit to sensibly investing their own money in public education' (National Commission on Terrorist Attacks 2004: 378).

Efforts to counter violent extremism in the Middle East and Africa have also come in the form of removing content from learning materials that is deemed to promote intolerance and violence. Whether it be glorifying or normalising violence and conflict or including content that fosters prejudice and intolerance against religious minorities (USCIRF 2016), countries such as Egypt, Afghanistan, and Pakistan have all reviewed and removed content from pre-existing classroom materials (Ghosh et al. 2016: 38–42). Saudi Arabia is another prominent example of a country that has been criticised for using teaching materials that encourage, 'hatred, intolerance and violence', and despite Saudi authorities disputing such allegations, there has been a national audit conducted by the Ministry of Education to ensure materials do not espouse intolerance and extremism (Ansary 2008: 126).

## Criticism and Critique

This chapter has considered an international cross-section of the diverse array of educational strategies in place across the globe designed to counter extremism, disrupt radicalisation, and reduce terrorism. The design and deployment of these initiatives differ quite significantly in places, but all could be accurately included under the heading 'CVE'. Broader peace-building and conflict resolution programmes have also been explored, and while these exhibit similarities and indeed have often influenced CVE programmes, they are more accurately considered as something distinct from CVE. The importance placed on CVE and education's role within it has increased significantly over the last two decades and, as with much of the GWOT, has not been without significant concern and criticism.

At the frontier of the GWOT, the criticism of CVE looks different to those focusing on the 'softer' approaches taken in the West. In the Middle East and North and East Africa, it has been argued that education has become 'another theatre in the War on Terror' where formal and non-formal schooling 'may be imbricated in a larger set of racialized counter-terrorist practices' (Shirazi 2017: 3–4). Education then becomes primarily related to the protection of the West and Western forces abroad and the furtherance of short-term foreign policy objectives rather than the security of local communities and long-term sustainable development (Novelli 2017: 841). However, criticisms of CVE deployed in the Global South by the West and those levelled at the CVE programmes used in the West may not be as far detached as first thought. As Novelli (2017) elaborates, education techniques and strategies tied to narrower security objectives in the South have been utilised in the West for management, monitoring, and control (see Chaps. 4 and 5).

For instance, one of the major criticisms of CVE in Western education concerns the formal expansion of the national security agenda into education and the way in which this frames students as simultaneously risky and at-risk as well as co-opting their educators into responsibilitised roles of surveillance, risk management, and reporting (McGhee 2010; Spiller et al. 2018). The theoretical and technical underpinnings of this approach have already been covered in Chaps. 3 and 4, but what critics argue here is that programmes of education put in place as a means of tackling extremism have also led 'to a range of concerns about the student/teacher relationship of trust, coupled with a concern that the security apparatus are increasingly policing education institutions, their actors and the contents of their classes' (Novelli 2017: 845).

These are oft-cited and important criticisms of the way in which CVE has expanded into education, but as Ford points out, 'while the surveillance role schools are increasingly playing has come under substantial critique, often the educational aspect is left unexamined' (Ford 2017: 147–148). Eschewing the more common line of critique, Ford hones in on some of the assumptions contained within dominant narratives around these programmes and their theories of change. For example, popular within dominant knowledge around CVE is the idea that education provides such tremendous potential because it provides a 'safe space' for the interrogation of close-minded extremist ideologies (UNESCO 2017: 22–24). Such ideas, Ford argues, rely on the notion that free speech is permissible and possible and that schools are physically protective of their students (Ford 2017: 149). However, standing in opposition to this reassuring notion is the reality that direct violence in the form of bullying, verbal abuse, and corporal punishment, the increasing presence of security apparatus within schools, forms of structural violence that perpetuate social inequality *and* increased surveillance in the classroom all pose serious questions of the 'safe space' narrative (Ford 2017: 149–150).

Problems pertaining to the deployment, environment, and indicative content may well be counter-productive to their stated objectives:

> I fear that these approaches, albeit unintentionally, might be driving young people towards 'extremism' rather than combatting it – through lack of reflexivity, humility, historical memory and nuance on the part of the architects and practitioners of CVE as they try to address this important issue. (Novelli 2017: 835–836)

Such fears speak to the argument that despite promoting a critical interrogation of the extremist ideologies that are so influential in the process of radicalisation, CVE initiatives within education are often designed to champion a hegemonic mono-cultural value set that not only risks alienating students but also undermines the extent to which this 'interrogation' is genuinely a critical one if the 'right answer' is known from the start and the process is one of shepherding students to this destination (Ford 2017:

150–151). Critical thought and critical investigation around controversial and difficult subject matter do not lend themselves to short-termism, prescription, and predetermined answers. Disagreement, contestation, frustration, and failure are things we should expect in these endeavours, and correspondingly we should be 'embracing doubt and uncertainty as essential aspects of education' (Passy and Haynes 2017: 162) and treating the classroom as a space for such experimentation and knowledge exchange. Doing things in this way has practical ramifications on pedagogical design as well classroom management because navigating such discussions is rarely easy but doing so would make the claim to promote critical thought a more honest one and respond to criticisms around securitising education (O'Donnell 2018; Thomas 2016).

## Conclusion

How a state responds to terrorism is of upmost importance in challenging it and reducing ensuing violence (English 2009). Government should be trying to avoid disproportionate responses that alienate and silence students, perpetuate structural violence, reduce genuinely critical discussions, and make counter-terrorism a formal responsibility of educators. Radicalisation has become increasingly pejorative, co-opted by the hegemonic GWOT discourse and linked to terrorism (Novelli 2017: 845), but this is a very contemporary and contested linkage that is only partially fixed. Education should be aiming to promote radicalisation among young people rather than being 'harnessed to the project of deradicalisation, under the banner of fighting Islamic terrorism' (Sukarieh and Tannock 2016: 22).

Education can foster the sort of radicalisation that lends itself to genuine open-mindedness and that recognises opportunities for radical social change and upheaval that redress social and structural inequality. Education that promotes peace and non-violence and that challenges extreme ideologies can have a progressive and positive impact on these goals, and this chapter has identified global initiatives that are doing just this, including those that are being led in regions suffering from ongoing violence or having recently transitioned into a post-conflict environment. If open and critical discussion in safe and inclusive spaces provides the opportunity to promote peace, social cohesion, and conflict management, then this should be the order of the day and the temptation to securitise the education of young people and young adults resisted.

## References

Ansary, A. F. 2008. "Combating extremism: a brief overview of Saudi Arabia's approach", *Middle East Policy*, 15(2): 111–142.

Bensalah Alaoui, A. 2017. "Morocco's security strategy: preventing terrorism and countering extremism", *European View*, 16(1): 103–120.

Brooks, C. 2017. "Enhancing conflict resilience of young Syrians", *Peace Review*, 29(2): 170–175.

Cook, S. A. 2008. "Give peace a chance: The diminution of peace in global education in the United States, United Kingdom, and Canada", *Canadian Journal of Education*, 31(4): 889–914.

Danesh, H. B. 2008. "The education for peace integrative curriculum: concepts, contents and efficacy", *Journal of Peace Education*, 5(2):157–173.

Danish Ministry of Immigration Integration and Housing. 2016. "Preventing and countering Extremism and Radicalisation". Available at: https://ec.europa.eu/home-affairs/sites/homeaffairs/files/what-we-do/networks/radicalisation_awareness_network/docs/preventing_countering_extremism_radicalisation_en.pdf

Davies, L. 2008. "Gender, education, extremism and security", *Compare: A Journal of Comparative and International Education*, 38(5): 611–625.

Davies, L. 2018. *Review of educational initiatives in counter-extremism internationally: what works?* Gothenburg: The Segerstedt Institute.

De Leede, S., Haupfleisch, R., Korolkova, K. and Natter, M. 2017. "*Radicalisation and violent extremism – focus on women: how women become radicalised and how to empower them to prevent radicalisation*". Available at: http://www.europarl.europa.eu/RegData/etudes/STUD/2017/596838/IPOL_STU(2017)596838_EN.pdf

Department of Education. 2013. "*Citizenship programmes of study: key stages 3 and 4*". Available at: https://assets.publishing.service.gov.uk/government/uploads/system/uploads/attachment_data/file/239060/SECONDARY_national_curriculum_-_Citizenship.pdf

Department of Education. 2018. "Schools, pupils and their characteristics: January 2018". Available at: https://assets.publishing.service.gov.uk/government/uploads/system/uploads/attachment_data/file/719226/Schools_Pupils_and_their_Characteristics_2018_Main_Text.pdf

Dutch Ministry of the Interior and Kingdom Relations. 2007. "Polarisation and radicalisation action plan 2007–2011". Available at: https://www.nyidanmark.dk/NR/rdonlyres/E9353925-A523-41C6-94F1-643EACF826CC/0/minbiz007_actieplanukv3.pdf

Educate Against Hate. 2018. "About". Available at: https://educateagainsthate.com/about/

Ellerby, K. 2013. "(En)gendered Security? The complexities of women's inclusion in peace processes", *International Interactions*, 39(4): 435–461.

English, W. 2009. *Terrorism and how to respond*. Oxford: Oxford University Press.

Enloe, C. H. 1990. *Bananas, beaches and bases: making feminist sense of international politics*. Berkeley, C.A.: University of California Press.

Ford, K. 2017. "Developing a peace perspective on counter-extremist education", *Peace Review*, 29(2): 144–152.

Fountain, S. 1999. *Peace education in UNICEF*. New York, N. Y.: UNICEF.

German Federal Government. 2016. *Federal government strategy to prevent extremism and promote democracy*. Berlin: Bundesministerium *für* Familie, Senioren, Frauen und Jugend.

Ghosh, R., Manuel, A., Chan, W.Y. A., Diliulati, M. and Babaei, M. 2016. "Education and Security: A Global Literature Review on the Role of Education in Countering Violent Extremism". Available at: https://institute.global/sites/default/files/inline-files/IGC_Education%20and%20Security.pdf

Ghosh, R. and Chan, Alice W.Y., Manuel, A. and Dilimulati, M. 2017. "Can education counter violent religious extremism?", *Canadian Foreign Policy Journal*, 23(3): 117–133.

Giscard d'Estaing, S. 2017 "Engaging women in countering violent extremism: avoiding instrumentalisation and furthering agency", *Gender and Development*, 25(1): 103–118.

Goetz, A. M. and Jenkins, R. 2016. "Agency and accountability: promoting women's participation in peacebuilding", *Feminist Economics*, 22(1): 211–236.

Gorbunova, J. 2016. "Modern information and educational environment: new possibilities of designing and implementing measures to counter extremist sentiments among the students", *Web of Conferences*, 29: 1–3.

Government Offices of Sweden. 2011. "*Action plan to safeguard democracy against violence promoting extremism*". Available at: https://www.government.se/contentassets/b94f163a3c5941aebaeb78174ea27a29/action-plan-to-safeguard-democracy-against-violence-promoting-extremism-skr.-20111244

Harris, I. M. 2004. "Peace education theory", *Journal of Peace Education*, 1(1): 5–20.

Hayes, S. W. 2017. "Changing radicalisation to resilience by understanding marginalisation", *Peace Review*, 29(2): 153–159.

Herrington, R. 2015. *Emerging practices in design, monitoring and evaluation of education for peace building programming*. Washington, D.C.: Search for Common Ground.

HM Government. 2011. *Prevent Strategy*. London: Stationary Office.

HM Government. 2015. *National Security Strategy and Strategic Defence and Security Review 2012: A Secure and Prosperous United Kingdom*. London: Stationary Office.

HM Government. 2018. *Contest: The United Kingdom's Strategy for Countering Terrorism*. London: Stationary Office.

Hudson, H. 2009. "Peacebuilding through a gender lens and the challenges of implementation in Rwanda and Côte d'Ivoire", *Security Studies*, 18(2): 287–318.

Hunt, S. 2002. "The critical role of women waging peace", *Columbia Journal of. Transnational Law*, 41(3): 557–572.

Lindborg, N. 2017. "The essential role of women in peacebuilding", *United States Institute of Peace*. Available at: https://www.usip.org/publications/2017/11/essential-role-women-peacebuilding

McGhee, D. 2010. *Security, citizenship and human rights: shared values in uncertain times.* Basingstoke: Palgrave Macmillan.

Ministère de l'Éducation et de l'Enseignement supérieur. 2018. "Ethics and Religious Culture Program". Available at: http://www.education.gouv.qc.ca/en/contenus-communs/parents-and-guardians/ethics-and-religious-culture-program/

Ministere de l'Education Nationale. 2015. "Grand mobilisation de l' école pour les valeurs de la République". Available at: http://cache.media.education.gouv.fr/file/02_-_fevrier/54/1/Grande-mobilisation-de-l-ecole-pour-les-valeurs-de-la-republique-lancement-des-assises_390541.pdf

Mirahmadi, H., Farooq, M. and Ziad, W. 2012. *Pakistan's civil society: alternative channels to countering violent extremism.* Washington, D.C.: WORDE.

Moffett, K. and Sgro, T. 2016. "School-based CVE strategies", *The Annals of the American Academy of Political & Social Science*, 668: 145–164.

Muslim Women's Network UK. 2018. "About Us". Available at: http://www.mwnuk.co.uk/

National Commission on Terrorist Attacks. 2004. *The 9/11 commission report.* New York, N. Y.: W.W. Norton & Company Inc.

National Coordinator for Security and Counterterrorism. 2016. "National coordinator for security and counterterrorism". Available at: https://english.nctv.nl/binaries/LR_100495_rapportage_EN_V3_tcm32-251878.pdf

Neumann, P. R. 2008. "Introduction". In P. R. Neumann, J. Stoil, & D. Esfandiary (eds.) *Perspectives on radicalisation and political violence: Papers from the first International Conference on Radicalisation and Political Violence.* London: ICSR: 3–7.

Novelli, M. 2017. "Education and countering violent extremism: western logics from south to north", *Compare*, 47(6): 835–851.

O'Donnell, A. 2018. "Contagious ideas: vulnerability, epistemic injustice and counter-terrorism in education", *Educational Philosophy and Theory*, 50(10): 981–997.

Passy, R. and Haynes, J. 2017. "Racism, Prevent and education: insisting on an open space", *Safer Communities*, 16(4): 155–165.

Rabasa, A., Pettyjohn, S. L., Ghez, J. J. and Boucek, C. 2010. *Deradicalizing islamist extremists.* Santa Monica, C.A.: RAND Cooperation.

Shirazi, R. 2017. "When schooling becomes a tactic of security: educating to counter "extremism"", *Diaspora, Indigenous, and Minority Education*, 11(1): 2–5.

Sjoberg, L. and Gentry, C. E. 2007. *Mothers, monsters and whores: women's violence in global politics*. London: Zed Books.

Spiller, K., Awan, I. and Whiting, A. 2018. "'What does terrorism look like?': university lecturers' interpretations of their Prevent duties and tackling extremism in UK universities", *Critical Studies on Terrorism*, 11(1): 130–150.

Subedi, DB. 2017. "Early warning and response for preventing radicalisation and violent extremism", *Peace Review*, 29(2): 135–143.

Sukarieh, M., and S. Tannock. 2016. "The deradicalisation of education: terror, youth and the assault on learning." *Race & Class* 57(4): 22–38.

Tamim, F. A. and Smith, S. M. 2010. "Human rights and insecurities: Muslims in post-9/11 East Africa". In Smith, Melinda, S. (ed.) *Securing Africa: post-9/11 discourses on terrorism*. London: Routledge: 99–125.

Taylor, E., Taylor, P. C., Karnovsky, S., Aly, A. and Taylor, N. 2017. ""Beyond Bali": a transformative education approach for developing community resilience to violent extremism", *Asia Pacific Journal of Education*, 37(2): 193–204.

Thomas, P. 2016. "Youth, terrorism and education: Britain's Prevent programme", *International Journal of Lifelong Education*, 35(2): 171–187.

Tickner, A. 2001. *Gendering world politics: issues and approaches in the post-Cold War era*. New York, N.Y.: Columbia University Press.

Vidino, L. and Brandon, J. 2012. "Europe's experience in countering radicalisation: approaches and challenges", *Journal of Policing, Intelligence and Counter-Terrorism*, 7(2): 163–179.

UNESCO. 2017. *Preventing violent extremism through education*. Available at: http://unesdoc.unesco.org/images/0024/002477/247764e.pdf

UNICEF. 2018. *Rights respecting schools award*. Available at: https://www.unicef.org.uk/rights-respecting-schools/

Universities UK. 2018. *Higher Education in numbers*. Available at: https://www.universitiesuk.ac.uk/facts-and-stats/Pages/higher-education-data.aspx

USCIRF. 2016. *Annual report*. Washington, D.C.: USCIRF.

Women Against Radicalisation Network. 2018. *What is Warn?*. Available at: https://warn.org.uk/what-is-warn/

Women Without Borders. 2018. *Homepage*. Available at: https://www.women-without-borders.org/

Zeiger, S. and Aly, A. 2015. *Countering violent extremism: developing an evidence base for policy and practice*. Abu Dhabi: Hedayah and Curtin University.

CHAPTER 7

# Investigating the Counter-Terrorism and Security Act in Higher Education

**Abstract** This chapter focuses on the Counter-Terrorism and Security Act (CTSA) and provides original empirical findings examining university lecturer perceptions of the new public duty within the CTSA. Emphasis is placed on the role of monitoring carried out by individuals as part of their job description—university lecturers monitoring their charges for indications of radicalisation or extremism. The chapter reviews the roles of university lecturers as an example of how public sector workers must perform the role of the security worker. As our findings demonstrate, there are tensions and contradictions felt by those mandated; for instance, a fear of not knowing when or how to report or even a no sense of defensive reporting—where due to the ambiguity in which the role of these duties are set, actors feel they must report all, for fear of repercussions. Equally, there are clear instances of resistance to how these newfound roles have been implemented and the challenges they instil to the freedoms and expectations that university lecturers hold dear.

**Keywords** Empirical findings • University lecturers • Deputisation • Resistance • Control workers

 
I. Awan et al., *Terrorism in the Classroom*, Palgrave Studies in Risk, Crime and Society,
https://doi.org/10.1007/978-3-030-01710-1_7

## Introduction

As we have argued in other chapters, the Counter-Terrorism and Security Act (CTSA) effectively asks those in positions of authority to monitor their supervisees. But what, we ask in this chapter, are the effects on those mandated to a national security regime with little or no security experience? And it is to the experiences of those working as university lecturers and those responsibilised to perform a Prevent Duty that we turn in this chapter. Our goal here is to document how those we spoke to comprehend and action their newfound security roles. In recent times, neoliberal approaches and economy models favouring privatisation, deregulation, and fiscal austerity have been readily applied to security, and this is evidenced through the wider spread of countering terror (see Heath-Kelly et al. 2015; Hoijtink 2014). The manner in which neoliberal values have also penetrated the field of education has helped to propel contentious issues arising from this new approach (see Baltodano 2012; Radice 2013)—for instance, unequal opportunities, an increasing audit culture, and the increasing educational and bureaucratic demands placed on academics (Mountz et al. 2015).

The government's decision to 'fast-track' the CTSA through parliament (House of Lords/House of Commons Joint Committee on Human Rights 2015) was met by criticism over the extent to which they allowed for proper scrutiny (see Independent 2016). The CTSA clearly entails an expansion of state roles of security into the educational sector (see Chap. 6), and our goal in this chapter is to establish lecturers' understandings of their CTSA roles. Given the then Home Secretary Theresa May's comments that educational staff 'should have sufficient training to be able to recognise vulnerability to being drawn into terrorism, and be aware of what action to take' (May 2015: 5), these individuals have a frontline responsibility. Underlying many of the issues we discuss in this chapter is the fact that there is no universal definition of the term radicalisation (as covered in Chap. 2); instead, there are a number of interpretations from policymakers, politicians, and academics. Therefore the interpretation of the CTSA and how lecturers react to the responsibilisation offer moments of contention and confusion.

In the aftermath of 9/11 and other terrorist atrocities, individuals and organisations have been increasingly enrolled into roles that may identify potential terrorism offenses (see Mueller and Stewart 2011). Those working in these roles have been labelled as 'control workers' or those making key decisions on those individuals pose particular risks (see Rose 2000). More often than not, this function is performed through categorisation; simply put, those that are calculated to be outside designated thresholds of acceptable risk are categorised as problematic (see Ericson and Haggerty 1997). These roles are more often than not performed with the assistance of automated and algorithmic systems that inform human decision-making (Gandy 2012). We contend that academics are 'control workers' because they now have security responsibilities due to the CTSA.

Within universities, management and staff have started to take a risk-averse approach to activities deemed controversial (Gardella 2006). This is a form of educational chilling where university management limits potential for risk, which, in turn, causes expectations and behaviours to be curtailed by those who have to seek approval to ask challenging questions (Palfreyman 2007). Moreover, when communities are labelled as 'suspect' or 'other', this has the undesirable effect of intensifying fears that often rely on stereotypes and heighten stigma towards specific populations (Mythen et al. 2009; Allen 2010; Spalek 2010; Awan 2012; Moosavi 2013; Mythen and Walklate 2006) (see Chaps. 3 and 6). Personifying these developments, and as has been noted by recent work on security, is a neoliberal agenda that responsibilises non-state actors into performing security roles (see Goold et al. 2010; Loader and Walker 2010; White 2011; Huysmans 2011) (see Chaps. 5 and 6). As mentioned in previous chapters, the UK governmental initiatives such as *Prevent* (2009), *Contest* (2011) or *Request a Check* (see Home Office 2014) encourage non-traditional participation by enrolling 'special' actors who are in effect deputised to perform security. The deputisation is mandated through the legislation and actors, be they frontline staff or designated staff, for instance, university lecturers reporting suspicious activity, and it is this agenda that we explore in relation to universities.

## Interviewing Lecturers

From April to November 2016, we conducted 20 interviews with university lecturers who were working in UK universities. The interviews were semi-structured and followed a loose script of five questions that was intended to ensure some consistency; these questions sought to establish awareness of CTSA duty, understanding of the CTSA, views on their universities response to the CTSA, and, lastly, document any personal experience of enacting the CTSA. Interviews were recorded and were conducted face-to-face, over the phone, via email, and using Skype. Once transcribed, the interviews were then coded and a thematic analysis was conducted. This was part of an ongoing reflective process where we each in turn read the transcripts offered as an initial set of themes. These were then further refined with additional rounds of reading and coding, and a number of themes across the transcripts were agreed upon. This informs our findings and the structure of the empirical sections that follow.

Those we interviewed included lecturers, senior lecturers, associate professors/readers, and professors. And the disciplinary spread included criminology, computer sciences, law, education, social science, business, and politics. Thirteen of the participants were male and seven female. Those interviewed worked in universities from across the UK. Our findings are far from exhaustive, given the size of our data set, and our work was explorative in nature, yet over 30 hours of interviews were recorded, which have produced a rich vein of information. More pressingly, when analysing the interviews, there was a clear saturation point, where key themes became evident (see Milliken 1999: 234). We remain aware that a larger sample size could have added additional themes, for example, of those we spoke to, none thought of their CTSA roles in a positive light. Nevertheless, what has emerged is a consensus as to how those we spoke to consider their CTSA role.

## The CTSA and the Role of Lecturers

Three prominent themes inform our findings: first, the responsibilising of lecturers and how lecturers understood their new CTSA role; second, defiance to the CTSA as articulated by lecturers; and third, chilling education or the risk-averse stances that universities are adopting towards the CTSA. We begin with responsibilising.

### *Responsibilising*

Lecturers' newfound role of monitoring students for expressions of radicalisation of extremism presents challenges to the founding qualities of university life, namely, intellectual freedoms. For participants the CTSA duty serves to undermine some of the core functions of the university. As one respondent put it:

> Its [University's] primary function is about debate, conduct of research, producing and disseminating knowledge and also dissent I think is really important. Universities should be a space for speaking truth to power [...] this kind of responsibility makes that far more difficult. (Politics, South East, Male)

Being duty-bound to evidence potential indicators of radicalisation or extremism, a lecturer undermines his understandings of academic freedoms (Lukianoff 2014) and indeed potentially hinders or curtails the topics students are comfortable discussing. The following participant continues:

> If I was expected to engage in significant monitoring of students it is likely that they (or at least some groups) would consider me to be a member of the state (or at least university) apparatus and be significantly more suspicious of me and cautious of what could be said. (Sociology, Yorkshire, Male)

To appear as a governmental operative, or indeed as a 'control worker', is not how this lecturer identifies, and indeed they once again find the CTSA as a means that will limit the potential of debate and discussion—inevitably students may shy away from difficult or loaded topics. For the following participant, freedoms of expressions are also of concern:

> How can we build trust with our students when the very thing we are doing will create suspicion and mistrust? I am genuinely not sure now whether someone wearing a headscarf or if someone has a beard should warrant me contacting the relevant services. I mean that's worrying because it's not just me who thinks like this. I have had colleagues contact me and say to me is she someone who needs reporting because she wears a face veil and has said she had travelled to Turkey for a holiday. (Social Sciences, East Midlands, Female)

Much like the commentary we have discussed in Chaps. 3 and 5, when securitising and identifying potential risks or 'risky' bodies, the selection process of categorising that risk or those that fit those criteria is problematic (Bausch and Zeitzoff 2015). Certain people or communities often feel a disproportionate sense of monitoring, persecution, or disadvantage (see McGovern and Tobin 2010; Choudhury and Fenwick 2011; Hickman et al. 2011). Universities, in principle, are founded on notions of speaking 'truth to power', and being mandated into a programme of surveillance is conflicting to the participants we spoke to, most especially as the focal lens of the CTSA does appear to be on the Muslim community, which in turn speaks to suspicion and mistrust of this particular population. All of this impacts knowledge production and the learning of staff and their students (Kyriacou et al. 2017).

A further aspect faced by lecturers is an unease and unknowing of how to react or intend what to do in terms of newfound responsibilities. Exacerbated by ambiguity around how to perform the Act (see Heath Kelly and Strausz 2018) heightens tensions and fears, which, as we argue, culminate in conservatism, anxieties, and resistance around doing something culpable (see Favarel-Garrigues et al. 2011; Power 2004). As the participant expands,

> we didn't have a strategy as an institution to deal with it so we were feeling around in the dark a little bit about how best to respond to the concerns that had been raised to us as academic staff and I think we probably took quite a risk averse approach… and I'm not suggesting that's necessarily a bad thing but I think that until we see some clearer guidance or guidelines around the sort of strategy that we should be adopting as an institution I think there are potential dangers and there are potential consequences for students and their futures if we are too risk averse and how we respond to any concerns that are raised. (Criminology, East Midlands, Male)

Being trained and being prepared are key ingredients to the successful implementation of the CTSA; however, of those we spoke to, none had received training. Instead, uncertainty remained as to the specifics of their roles, that is, what they are expected to do. Equally, the language of CTSA document, they felt, was ambiguous and served to heighten their sense of frustration and resistance to the programme, as will be evident in the following section.

### *Defiance*

The CTSA has added to already stretched and overloaded university staff workloads (see Mountz et al. 2015), and this too may add to the reluctance of staff to engage with the CTSA. Not only are they unsure of what to do, but they are committed to other teaching, research, and administrative tasks, a phenomenon that is echoed in other settings such as the NHS (see Heath-Kelly and Strausz 2018). Some of the dangers of deputising staff without the requisite skills and training are addressed directly by one of our participants:

> Staff are just simply not qualified to do this, academic staff are not psychologists or psychiatrists, they're not counter-terrorist practitioners, they're frequently overworked and balancing multiple responsibilities. There is something particularly dangerous I think about asking staff to become involved in these kind of matters. (Politics, South East, Male)

On account of this, for many, the CTSA imposes responsibilities that go beyond their duties as educators and this occasionally provokes moments of resistance: 'I am not going to deal with [CTSA]... I will not report something, but if I know a person is going to plant a bomb, then yes, I will call the police' (Law, South East, Female). In this excerpt the lecturer makes apparent that she will not be reporting unless there is a clear danger, the motivations lying with a broader civil duty rather than the CTSA.

These utterances demonstrate fractious moments of localised resistance but may speak to what Scott (2013) calls 'anarchist calisthenics', whereby people must practise small examples of everyday resistance in order to be prepared for moments of more serious or sustained resistance. Low-level disobedience such as 'jaywalking' or crossing the road when it is clear and the red pedestrian light is showing help to reduce the fear one may feel in resisting different forms of power down the line. Within this conceptual frame, the localised resistance we witness from lecturers can be understood as a tentative form of protest that may well pave the way for more significant forms of resistance. However, framing these individual actions (or non-actions) as such may be overly optimistic, and others have certainly pointed towards what they consider a passivity from universities in their adoption of neoliberal approaches to education and their acceptance of education's role in furthering counter-terrorism efforts (Mountz et al. 2015; Radice 2013). Indeed, the two go hand in hand, as within a broader context of neoliberal education we have come to expect increasing workloads and additional responsibility placed on academics. The security function academics are now expected to carry out represents another example of this trend, albeit one that is fairly unprecedented, and exposes the tentative and awkward reasoning they apply to their newfound responsibilities.

Whether we take heart from the moments of disobedience or lament the passivity of HE, our research implies that this is not something that academics feel they have the skillset to accomplish nor do they see it as part of their fundamental role as educators or as the fundamental purpose of university. Instead, it presents another example of the pressure of the 'neo-liberal university' taking precedent (see Ball 2012) as one lecturer highlights in relation to free speech within their department:

> I think people think very strongly about it, and I think, you know [University] has a reputation for being radical political place. I think it would totally undermine our sort of, core bits of our identity if we were suddenly trying to squash debate in that way. (Politics, South East, Female)

The department mentioned here was once celebrated for its radical views that date back to its Marxist positioning in the 1970s and 1980s and which allowed it to challenge political convention of the time. This lecturer feels that the positive, critical heritage that the department has cultivated is under threat by this governmental mandate. On a broader level, the freedom to challenge and debate is typically viewed as a central component of HE and of departments across the country (Royed 1996), a characteristic that is contested by the arrival of the CTSA and that may undermine the role of the lecturer and securitise the institution and those enrolled in it:

> I think the main role of a university is in the development of a critical outlook both inside and outside of its walls (partly) through the generation of new knowledge. I do not see it as a disciplinary agent (aside from within the academic disciplines themselves). It should certainly not be a tool of state surveillance indeed it should have the potential to encourage dissent. I don't believe that the university has any special role in this and individuals within the university do not have any particular responsibility in this over and above any individuals in society. We all have a responsibility for the welfare of others. (Sociology, Yorkshire, Male)

In the face of these grievances and misgivings that are being felt by lecturers in relation to the duty imposed upon them, we contend that evidence suggesting decisions to dismiss the duty or simply 'pay lip service' to it offers some understanding of how resistance and defiance are manifesting. While distinct to the broader institutional responses that will be covered below, such behaviour provides illustrative examples of the most readily available forms of resistance that are being practised by academics.

### *Chilling Education*

There may be a deep-seated understanding felt by lecturers that universities are overly cautious in their interpretations of CTSA. This, as we have suggested, may be due to perceived challenges on intellectual freedoms, but also evident is animosity to the defensive approaches taken by the universities. As a result, there are problematic issues in relation to how individuals feel a sense of fear and anxiety. For example, this has translated to a 'paranoia surrounding ongoing events within the university' (Sociology, West Midlands, Female), which has also led to bureaucratic practices in relation to the vetting of external speakers at university events. As a participant explains,

> We tried to organise a conference and invited a number of guest speakers. However, we had to fill in all these forms and once we completed them the University rejected our application. We were never told why except that the list of speakers and event I think was too sensitive, because it was about terrorism. (Sociology, Midlands, Male)

This also shows how this particular participant felt that there are particular issues because of the sensitivities regarding debate and education. For example, this also means that this could be problematic for student and supervisor relationship:

> It...feels a bit awkward, for instance I have Saudi PhD student and I always have to reminder her that if she is going away, she has to notify the authorities, everything she needs to do she has got to ask permission in a way that other students don't. And I feel a bit apologetic about it and you know, a little bit like I am part of this system that doesn't trust her. It is quite minor. I certainly don't feel scared or suspicious of students, I don't think. (Education, South West, Female)

The problem in relation to Brexit and matters related later also reveal that some students may face greater scrutiny as a result. This means that students potentially are stigmatised because of their nationality.

One more factor to consider is the role of the ethics committee and gaining ethical clearance. For example, the participant in the following excerpt notes the problems with gaining ethical clearance because of the CTSA duty:

> Ethics reviews are more difficult doing this kind of research. But I guess it show ups the difficulties of ethical review processes, because if you are doing research on far right extremist websites that actually ethics is a constant negotiation rather than a review that happens at one point in time and then is kind of dealt with. I think it also about the relationship with the person, so the student has a history of involvement in anti-racist practice…So I guess it is about knowing the project I have and the risk of radicalisation through exposure to these spaces and I also think it is really important to have the freedom to go on these spaces and understand these space. Because how are you going to combat things like racism, it is important to understand how these ideologies are produced, how they circulate, how they are consumed. (Geography, Scotland, Male)

Postgraduate students face a further problem in relation to the contribution to knowledge factor, which means potentially researching sensitive topics that are likely to cause difficulties. The ethics committee therefore may be seen as a barrier towards the types of research that have a counter-productive effect (Pruzan 2016). The evaluation process and the historical nature of building a case for the ethical clearance can be time-consuming.

The notion that such policies may also lead to counter-productive assertions about the research was likely to cause immediate tensions between how to interpret the policy and how to ensure that it is a fair process:

> The question with a general policy statement like that is how will universities translate into practice and I'm sure you'll find that there are many different attitudes and approaches across different universities. You might get some that follow it quite slavishly you might get some that pay lip service to it and don't really buy into the underlying ethos and you might get some that frankly don't pay any regard to it at all. (Law, Wales, Male)

This shows that the education sector as a whole is not a homogenous institution, and that it is, in fact, being pushed by central government to tackle counter-terrorism. For example, the idea that some institutions, such as Oxford and Cambridge debating societies, are exempt from the 'extremist speakers' ban reveals the problems with the policy in practice (Espinoza 2015).

The CTSA and responses to it add additional responsibilities to teaching staff in how they monitor their charges, but also additional pressures about how potential sensitive material is handled. In the following case, initiating training on countering radicalisation appears to be an ill-conceived response to a complaint about teaching materials.

> One person I know was required to take the (Prevent) training because a student complained about her use of some radical cartoons in class (presumably she explained the problems therein but the student either did not understand it was being used for educative reasons or they were offended for other reasons). She was not penalised for using the cartoons as such, because it was recognised that her use was not a violation of anything we sign up for in teaching responsibilities, but she was asked to take the training anyway. She indicated to me that the trainer was very ambivalent about the materials they were teaching and seemed to believe that much of what was being taught was very problematic and unreconstructed. I found that interesting, an obvious tension in the policy at the ground level that apparently wasn't taken into consideration or is not considered important. Once again we are being told as professional educators that we don't know what we are doing. What do 'they' expect? (Law, South East, Female)

Using Prevent training as a vehicle of awareness towards how to teach is outside of the remit of what the CTSA may be hoping to achieve, and again this may help highlight the misapplication of the Act and how it is interpreted. As the participant highlights, the ambivalence of trainers towards the Act and what they were teaching influences the application of the training. Equally using the training as a form of discipline as to how university lecturers are using their course material may once again infringe on senses of free speech. In this instance, the training and its delivery may have had the effect of disenfranchising the lecture, and the participant who spoke to us, from the CTSA and what it is attempting to achieve. In addition, if lecturers feel they cannot use certain material, their activities may become curtailed by avoiding using what they understand to be illegitimate materials.

Providing a duty of care to students or ensuring their well-being is key to the role of universities. There is an argument to suggest universities as space where young and passionate people should be free to express their opinions. But equally, students and other members of society are frequently impressionable or susceptible to influence. Nevertheless, the CTSA is an expansion of state-led security into the educational sector, and our goal has been to establish how lecturers understand their CTSA roles and to document their thoughts on the duty. As the following lecturer suggests,

> We have to be sensitive to any signs of radical tendencies or concepts amongst students. It is not always easy though – radicalisation frequently occurs as a silent process that happens gradually without any external signals. If we see any signs of it – we should either confront or possibly report it for further evaluation (I could be wrong, so this would have to be a careful process). (Data science, South England, Male)

Indeed, perhaps universities are already doing this through their pastoral care:

> Every time a student comes through your door with a concern … you have got to ask personal questions, you have got to challenge certain types of behaviour … Would I go so far as reporting someone [to Channel programme], I do not know. … in the same way that if I had a student in a seminar that I think is going through some difficulties, I will report them to a student support manager. (Criminology, North England, male)

Despite the threats posed by terrorism acts, there are clear issues in relation to making it a legal requirement to instigate students as potential extremists. In this way, HE institutions must now start to hold an open and honest debate about the right of students and academics. Universities are places where freedom of expression is supposed to flourish and not be stifled by practices that mean academics lose the trust of their students.

## The Academic Community

In what remains of the chapter we want to offer three points in expanding how we may begin to understand the impacts of CTSA in UK universities. First, we consider the role of responsibilising. This for us mirrors previous work on the 'control worker' as this is effectively a role lecturers must perform and they must make authoritative decisions on potential risk factors (Rose 2000; Ericson and Haggerty 1997). This is evidenced in having to seek permissions for invited speakers and gaining permissions from senior management—perhaps, lectures limit their selections to those they know or suspect will gain approval. Therefore the control in the first instance is with the lecturer and how subconsciously or consciously they make their decision. Factored is the CTSA, 'sensitive' topics, and ones undoubtedly linked to terrorism or extremism, yet the overarching tone and climate of this kind of selection process cultivates fear and suspicion around pertinent social debates and discussions. Moreover a climate of fear may pervade senior management as they seek avoid adverse publicity in curtailing knowledge production and indeed greater understanding of the issues that are stigmatising certain UK communities and populations (see Guardian 2015).

As we stress, universities lecturers are increasingly being tasked with security responsibilities, for instance, monitoring student attendance or being attentive to the visas their student have and it is these responsibilities that acclimatise student and lecturers to the mandate (cf. Caplan 2011). There can be no doubt that record-keeping is a necessary element of organisational life and the function of a university; indeed, records of exam results speak to this. However, in our institution, we must record attendance at all seminars and lectures—and this is done by students signing their name on a sheet—and then after class lecturers must enter this into a database. In this way, we monitor students and are well-practised in surveilling (indeed, adding a student's attitude or style of dress as the CTSA's 22 Framework pinpoints is something that could be easily added to lecturing roles). There are indicators of risk (Deleuze 1992), and policing in such a way regulates how we deal with students; if a number of absences are recorded, then it starts processes and procedures to arrest those absences or expel the student. These skills are transferable and are readily used to manage risk, and it must be stressed that they are a necessary component of university functionality. The CTSA's 22 Framework offers indicator that informs the decisions of 'control workers' that ultimately record, categorise, and designate advantage.

Second, as we have seen, university lecturers are presenting their own forms of little resistances or everyday defiance. Through acts of ignoring, feigning ignorance, or even cursory responses, lecturers are to some degree appeasing their own disgruntlement with their roles in the CTSA. In addition, more formalised response has also been presented in the form of open letters to national newspapers (Guardian 2016), and indeed Universities UK and the UUC (the largest HE union) have taken a more than sceptical stance towards the CTSA. Nevertheless, no large objection to the Act has been lodged by universities or their staff, and these small defiance may be more informative as to how staff are responding to its demands.

Third, chilling education is a perspective of compliance which overrides the day-to-day running of universities; in this case there is an inherent conservatism with regard to anything that could be construed as controversial. Indeed, within universities there are designated groups whose purpose is the successful implementation of the CTSA. These 'Prevent Groups' are management-led, but also involve teaching staff, and they lead on aspects such as Prevent Training and establishing management protocols in the face of potential instances of extremism or radicalisation (Qurashi (2017). Such an approach is centred on an organisational response, where protocols are rarely challenged, but the emphasis is on performing the monitoring task placed upon the university. In an age where auditing pressures and fear of litigation are omnipresent, compliance to such demands, it appears, outweighs a greater understanding of what is being asked or indeed any challenges that could or should be levied at the responsibility. As we have documented, lecturers are clear that their universities are defensive, at the very least, in their interpretation of the CTSA. Underpinning this view are concerns about disruptions to intellectual freedom and conflicts with duties of care and pastoral etiquette.

## Conclusion

In this chapter we have discussed university lecturers' interpretations of the responsibility they face in their CTSA roles. As we have seen, the CTSA can hinder opportunities to engage in open debate, restricting research around 'sensitive' topics and creating a divide between staff as surveillants and students as potential risk takers. The argument here is not intended to highlight that lecturers are frequently spread thin across a range of diverse roles but, instead, that these extra statutory duties combined with a sense of ambiguity around the specifics of these duties could, in fact, be dangerous as well as counter-productive. And it is something the lecturers we spoke to are ill at ease with performing. In Chap. 8, we will draw upon the findings of this chapter and the points raised in preceding chapters to offer an overview of what we have discussed and to present our concluding points.

## References

Allen, C. 2010. Islamophobia. London: Ashgate Publishing.

Awan, I. 2012. "'I'm a Muslim Not an Extremist:' How the Prevent Strategy Has Constructed a 'Suspect' Community." Politics & Policy 40 (6): 1158–1185.

Ball, S. J. 2012. "Performativity, Commodification and Commitment: An I-Spy Guide to the Neoliberal University." British Journal of Educational Studies 60 (1): 17–28.

Baltodano, M. 2012. "Neoliberalism and the Demise of Public Education: The Corporatization of Schools of Education. International." Journal of Qualitative Studies in Education 25 (4): 487–507.

Bausch, A. W., and T. Zeitzoff. 2015. "Citizen Information, Electoral Incentives, and Provision of Counter-Terrorism: An Experimental Approach." Political Behavior 37 (3): 723–748.

Caplan, J. 2011. "The Administration of Gender Identity in Nazi Germany." History Workshop Journal 72: 171–180.

Choudhury, T., and H. Fenwick 2011. "The Impact of Counter-Terrorism Measures on Muslim Communities." Equality and Human Rights Commission Research Report 72. Accessed 20 June 2016. http://www.equalityhumanrights.com/uploaded_files/research/counter-terrorism_research_report_72.pdf

Deleuze, G. 1992. "Postscript on the Societies of Control." October 59, 3–7.

Ericson, R. V., and K. D. Haggerty. 1997. Policing the Risk Society. Oxford: OUP.

Espinoza, J. 2015. "Oxford and Cambridge Debating Societies Escape Ban on Extremism." The Telegraph, Accessed 16 March 2015. http://www.telegraph.co.uk/education/universityeducation/student-life/11471654/Oxford-and-Cambridge-debating-societies-escape-ban-on-extremism.html

Favarel-Garrigues, G., T. Godefroy, and P. Lascoumes. 2011. "Reluctant Partners? Banks in the Fight against Money Laundering and Terrorism Financing in France." Security Dialogue 42 (2): 179–196.

Gandy, O. H. 2012. Coming to Terms with Chance: Engaging Rational Discrimination and Cumulative Disadvantage. London: Ashgate Publishing.

Gardella, T. M. 2006. "Beyond Terrorism: The Potential Chilling Effect on the Internet of Broad Law Enforcement Legislation." John's L Reviews 80: 655.

Goold, B., I. Loader, and A. Thumala. 2010. "Consuming Security? Tools for a Sociology of Security Consumption." Theoretical Criminology 14 (3): 3–30. doi:https://doi.org/10.1177/1362480609354533.

Guardian. 2015. "Mohammed Emwazi's University Suspends All 'Sensitive' Events." The Guardian, Accessed 27 February 2015. https://www.theguardian.com/education/2015/feb/27/mohammed-emwazi-university-westminster-refuses-to-cancel-preacher-talk-islamic-society

Guardian. 2016. "Anti-Radicalisation Strategy Lacks Evidence Base in Science." The Guardian. Accessed 29 September 2016. https://www.theguardian.com/politics/2016/sep/29/anti-radicalisation-strategy-lacks-evidence-base-in-science

Heath-Kelly, C. and Strausz, E. 2018. Counterterrorism in the NHS: Evaluating Prevent Duty Safeguarding. Available at https://www.docdroid.net/boB68fG/counter-terrorism-in-the-nhs.pdf

Heath-Kelly, C., C. Baker-Beall, and L. Jarvis. 2015. "Editors' Introduction: Neoliberalism And/As Terror." Critical Studies on Terrorism 8 (1): 1–14.

Hickman, J., L. Thomas, S. Silvestri, and H. Nickels, 2011. "Suspect Communities: Counter-Terrorism Policy, the Press and the Impact on Irish and Muslim Communities in Britain." Accessed 9 January 2017. http://www.statewatch.org/news/2011/jul/uk-london-met-suspect-communitiesfindings.pdf.

Hoijtink, M. 2014. "Capitalizing on Emergence: The 'New' Civil Security Market in Europe." SecurityDialogue 45 (5): 458–475.

Home Office. 2014. Request a Check. Accessed 20 August 2016 https://eforms.homeoffice.gov.uk/outreach/righttowork.ofml

House of Lords/House of Commons Joint Committee on Human Rights. 2015. "Legislative Scrutiny:Counter-Terrorism and Security Bill." Fifth Report of Session 2014–2015, Accessed 20 August 2016. http://www.publications.parliament.uk/pa/jt201415/jtselect/jtrights/86/86.pdf

Huysmans, J. 2011. "What's in an Act? On Security Speech Acts and Little Security Nothings." Security Dialogue 42 (4/5): 371–383.

Independent. 2016. "New Counter-Extremism Strategy Could Make Fight Even Harder." MPs warn. Accessed July 21 2016. http://www.independent.co.uk/news/uk/politics/counter-extremism-prevent-strategy-could-make-fight-even-harder-a7149351.html

Kyriacou, C., R. Szczepek, B. Beatrice, F. Said, and I. Davies. 2017. "British Muslim University Students' Perceptions of Prevent and Its Impact on Their Sense of Identity." Education, Citizenship and Social Justice 12 (2): 97–110.

Loader, I., and N. Walker. 2010. Civilising Security. Cambridge: Cambridge University Press.

Lukianoff, G. 2014. Freedom from Speech. New York: Encounter Books.

May, T. 2015. Home Secretary: We must work together to defeat terrorism. Available at https://www.gov.uk/government/speeches/home-secretary-we-must-work-together-to-defeat-terrorism

McGovern, M., and A. Tobin 2010. "Countering Terror or Counter-Productive: Comparing Irish and British Muslim Experiences of Counter-Insurgency" Law and Policy, Report of a Symposium held in Cultúrlann McAdam Ó Fiaich, Falls Road, Belfast. 23–24 June 2009.

Milliken, S. 1999. "The Study of Discourse in International Relations: A Critique of Research and Methods." European Journal of International Relations 5 (2): 225–254.

Moosavi, L. 2013. "Islamophobia in the Representations of Islam and Muslims by the British Government between 2001 and 2007." Turkish Journal of Sociology 27 (3): 33–368.

Mountz, A., A. Bonds, B. Mansfield, J. Loyd, J. Hyndman, M. Walton-Roberts, and W. Curran. 2015. "For Slow Scholarship: A Feminist Politics of Resistance through Collective Action in the Neoliberal University." ACME: An International Journal for Critical Geographies 14 (4): 1235–1259.

Mueller, J., and M. G. Stewart. 2011. Terror, Security, and Money: Balancing the Risks, Benefits, and Costs of Homeland Security. Oxford: Oxford University Press.

Mythen, G., and Walklate, S. 2006. Beyond The Risk Society: Critical Reflections On Risk And Human Security: Critical Reflections on Risk and Human Security. London: McGraw-Hill Education.

Mythen, G., S. Walklate, and F. Khan. 2009. "'I'm a Muslim, but I'm Not a Terrorist': Victimization, Risky Identities and the Performance of Safety." The British Journal Of Criminology 49: 736–754.

Palfreyman, D. 2007. "Is Academic Freedom under Threat in UK and US Higher Education?" Education and the Law 19 (1): 19–40.

Power, M. 2004. The Risk Management of Everything: Rethinking the Politics of Uncertainty. London: Demos.

Pruzan, P. 2016. Research Methodology: The Aims, Practices and Ethics of Science. New York: Springer International Publishing.

Qurashi, F. 2017. "Just Get on with It: Implementing the Prevent Duty in Higher Education and the Role of Academic Expertise." Education, Citizenship and Social Justice, First Online.

Radice, H. 2013. "How We Got Here: UK Higher Education under Neoliberalism". ACME: An International. Journal for Critical Geographies 12 (2): 407–418.

Rose, N. 2000. "Government and Control." British Journal of Criminology 40 (2): 321–339.

Royed, T. J. 1996. "Testing the Mandate Model in Britain and the United States: Evidence from the Reagan and Thatcher Eras." British Journal of Political Science 26 (01): 45–80.

Scott, J. C. 2013. Two Cheers for Anarchism: Six Easy Pieces on Autonomy, Dignity, and Meaningfuln Work and Play. Princeton: Princeton University Press.

Spalek, B. 2010. "Community Policing, Trust, and Muslim Communities in Relation to New Terrorism." Politics & Policy 38 (4): 789–815.

White, A. 2011. "The New Political Economy of Private Security." Theoretical Criminology 16 (1): 85–101.

CHAPTER 8

# Conclusion

**Abstract** This chapter offers concluding comments on the main issues that have informed the book as well as those that have emerged from it. We first offer an overview of key themes raised in the previous chapters before discussing the emerging critical voice toward Prevent in UK Higher Education. We then argue for the need for greater transparency, specifically in relation to the encroachment of counter-extremism within education and the effects it has, and also on a broader level with regard to the evidence and thought that underpin the government's entire approach. We draw the book to a close by offering our final thoughts and reflections on what the formal expansion of counter-extremism means to us as university lecturers.

**Keywords** Reflections • Transparency • Contest • Freedom of information

## Introduction

In previous chapters we have discussed key issues relating to the Prevent Strategy and its effects on education in the UK, and in this (our final) chapter, we offer some concluding comments on the themes that have emerged from our findings. We begin the chapter by contemplating the issues we have raised in each chapter, and then move to consider the



I. Awan et al., *Terrorism in the Classroom*, Palgrave Studies in Risk, Crime and Society,
https://doi.org/10.1007/978-3-030-01710-1_8

growing attention the strategy is attracting in relation to HE. Following this, we argue for the need for greater transparency in relation to UK counter-extremism both within education and more broadly in relation to the evidence and thought that underpin the entire strategy. Finally, we present some reflective thoughts on why the work of the book is important in furthering knowledge of Prevent as understood by those who are responsibilised by it to perform security roles.

## Reflecting on Emergent Themes

The first theme we consider is ambiguity of language, never more pressing than in the definition that surrounded the Strategy. As Chap. 2 contends, there is a lack of precision in the language used throughout the Strategy, and this has the effect of confusing those who have to enact the Strategy—that is, lecturers. Indeed, in the context of education, a broader spectrum of issues such as foreign policy, self-identity issues, and/or problems of integration have helped to confuse how radicalisation and extremism (or terrorism) are defined in relation to a setting such as HE. At best the definitions of radicalisation and extremism remain vague, and their emergence in the HE setting as part of a counter-extremism strategy has raised questions as to how the government is deploying them to justify the mandating of particular actions. We are not suggesting these definitions are completely without merit; however, when they are used to cover a wide and imprecise range of factors and consequently where political acts or specific cultural/religious identifiers have the potential to be associated with violence, extremism, and terrorism, there are clearly broader concerns. Central to our observations is the problem of interpretation, especially when this is used to identify vulnerabilities and safeguarding against extremist threats.

We have also examined the development of policy and responses to terrorism in the UK. Evident here has been the spectre of 9/11 and the terrorist events that have followed, such as the 2017 attacks in Westminster and London Bridge in the UK. Indeed, one commends the government's response in the face of such attacks and in updating their strategy, as was done in May 2018 to respond to a changing threat as well as to criticism. However, what does remain in these policies and their implementation are some of the concerns of old that have undoubtedly had the effect of castigating certain populations in the UK as 'other' (see Said 1995). As we have contended, the position of vigilance in schools is often accompanied with a language of 'Britishness' where students and teachers alike are expected to promote and uphold an ill-defined set of hegemonic mono-cultural values (Ford 2017: 150–151).

The promotion of 'British Values' demands a stable and clear definition (which does not currently exist), and in its absence, such an approach threatens to alienate sections of the population. As we attest, there are few aspects in these values that are unique to Britain, and while 'British Values' do appear in the new CONTEST strategy, the appearance of the more generic 'shared values' and 'values of our society' alongside it perhaps indicates that the government wishes to move away from what has been an area oft-targeted for criticism (HM Government 2018). This is a poorly conceived reactionary device used in HE to counter terrorism, but in doing so, it draws on tensions that exist towards certain communities in the UK. As we have considered in Chap. 3, the issue of suspect communities is very much evident in the UK, and when specific groups are subject to heightened attention, sensations of persecution and alienation prevail, especially when the language used to motivate the approach is ambiguous and open to interpretation. The detrimental impact of such an approach on community relations is detrimental to broader cohesion, and in countering terrorism or crime, most often such an approach acerbates problems (Hilyard 1993).

What can also be added to this aspect of suspiciousness is monitoring with the goal of controlling those groups. Indeed, as we argue in Chap. 4, surveillance and monitoring per se is a structuring principle, and it offers data and information that are useful in countering terrorism as well as the efficient running of an organisation. Nevertheless, it is the interpretation of how risks are evaluated, understood, and presented to HE staff that is a prescient concern. The Prevent Strategy gives rise, reason, and authority to how institutions such as universities monitor their charges and make decisions on possible radicalisation or terrorist intent. As Chap. 4 argues, there is a mature literature on surveillance practice and its consequences and unintended consequences, and what we have done here is drawn upon some of this literature that highlights how those in positions of civil authority must surveil their charges for potential misdeeds. Indeed, the growing phenomenon of private and public blurring in matters of security further complicates just how some of this work is structured and its result in securing its intended purpose (see Ball et al. 2015), particularly when monitoring contributes to inequalities or lack of transparency (Gandy 2012).

Underlying the observation we have made in this book are notions of power and control, for this is the pre-eminent reasoning of the Prevent Strategy—to control those who wish to conduct acts of terrorism and to influence or guide those at risk of extremism or radicalisation. As we have argued, constructions of risk have lubricated the implementation of the Prevent Strategy, and here we have turned to Foucault, amongst others, to consider responses to risk. There are clear political motives in the rhetoric that surrounds the Strategy, and indeed the recent emotive language of 'hearts and minds' used by the Home Secretary further evidences how the debate is being structured. Yet, as we have suggested, terrorism provides the seminal object within the dispostif of precautionary risk and its very existence is pre-empted on a fallacy of countering the possibility of unknowns. Indeed, this is the difficulty the government faces; even with high levels of intelligence, many of the recent acts of terror have been committed by those 'unknown to the security services'. Therefore the knowledge base upon which the Strategy sits overextends the real evidence upon which it is based. Instead, the Prevent Strategy offers the illusion that the government is controlling the uncontrollable (Beck 2002). Key to our consideration of discourses surrounding Prevent is a lack of evidence for governmental claims that contain a number of intuitive sounding but unsubstantiated assumptions (further discussed below). No doubt the task faced by the security forces is an unenviable one, yet the justification and positioning of the Prevent Strategy, its governance, and indeed the role of university lecturers in its application further muddy a logic that is built on ambiguous definitions.

In Chap. 6, we offer some perspective on how those outside the UK are dealing with threats of terrorism, radicalisation, and extremism. Key here has been governmental responses to terrorism and considerations of balance, as disproportionate reactions are often counterproductive and alienate or antagonise those subject to new laws, policy, or declarations. What we have considered is educational settings and their role in promoting peace, challenging extremism and countering terrorism. Education, we stress, should encourage a form of radical thought that embraces open-mindedness and tolerance and serves as a driving force to promote peace, non-violence, and challenge to extreme ideologies. Yet, as we draw on in Chap. 6, there is a concern that educational spaces are in danger of becoming another theatre in the War on Terror, where students and staff, as well as associates, become part of a larger mandate. As we have demonstrated, it is the formal expansion of security into educational settings and the framing of students as risky, as well as co-opting educators into responsibilised roles of surveillance, risk management, and reporting (McGhee 2010; Spiller et al. 2018) that present much to be considered.

The final theme that the book has sought to highlight is an empirical understanding of Prevent in HE. In doing so, we have been struck by how lecturers have responded to their roles and the culture of fear as well as moments of resistance that may be incipient in HE. As Chap. 7 has discussed, there is a deep-seated unease felt by university lecturers in what they have been asked to do. This stems from three main dispositions: first, a reluctance to participate in the act of being responsibilised into a security role; second, and relatedly, compromises made to their pastoral positions or being viewed as governmental agents; and finally, curtailments to perceived freedom of expression. In the third instance, a freedom to discuss or research any given topic is a prerequisite to learning and university life, and to have to be mindful of what one is focusing on against the backdrop of a statutory duty, as we have found, operates contrary to these intellectual pursuits. Indeed, in a climate of the 'Neoliberal University' where expectations and increasing responsibilities are levied onto teaching staff, alongside other academic pressures (Ball 2012), growing pressures are having detrimental impacts on university life. A culture of fear may be pervading how staff are dealing with sensitive issues such as Islamophobia or right-wing extremism. Additionally, being reponsibilised by the state to perform a security function runs counter to the traditional function of the university, and as such, lecturers have expressed to us how a dissatisfaction with this has manifested in moments of resistance to these forms of control and power. Of course, there is a more complex landscape to this, and as we have made clear, there is a requirement that staff do their utmost to maintain the safety of students; however, it is the proportionality of Prevent Duty that, we argue, goes too far and engenders counter-productive results.

## Growing Critical Voice

Our position in this book has taken a critical perspective on the role of Prevent and the CTSA in education and is not unique in this regard. There have been persistent concerns raised by a growing coterie of commentators, many of whom have been drawn upon in this book, that speak to various aspects of the UK's counter-terrorism strategy. Their focus, and ours, inevitably concentrates on the concepts that underpin these

Strategies, but also the consequence as to how they impact on HE and UK society. Education, after all, is central to gaining knowledge and providing students with key skills that should include the ability to reason, debate, and challenge pre-existing dogmas. Nonetheless, what recent observations have suggested is that education is increasingly being used as a vehicle to undermine the challenges faced by wider society. Indeed, O'Donnell's (2017, 2018) observations, drawing on Foucault (2007), Arendt (1961), and Fricker (2007), highlight the preposterousness of Prevent in UK education, and she is forceful in attesting that securitisation and political impetuses should remain absent from how education is conceptualised and indeed delivered to students. There is a rigidity to how Prevent and the CTSA have been applied to education that simply undermines the alternative voice or shapes how 'others' may be interpreted and understood—an aspect that can be readily viewed through constructs of 'suspect communities'. A key point O'Donnell makes is *pedagogical injustice* which undermines the teacher's personal judgement and relies on 'codified rules' that present linear and blinkered perspectives. As she elaborates,

> *the student is understood not simply as knower but as learner; the professional judgement of the teacher can be undermined either by systematically doubting one's own judgement and perceptions because of being asked to read statements and contributions from students through a lens of a security agenda or by applying codified rules, such as looking for crude indicators of radicalisation; teachers may feel caught between competing demands: to respond ethically to the student by being a virtuous hearer and being compelled to deploy social stereotypes and identity prejudice (which they may not hold themselves) by enacting the Prevent duty.* (O'Donnell 2017: 179)

The logic to Prevent and CTSA in the classroom is to provide a clear agenda of how to identify risk or vulnerability and to teach what is wrong. Yet, many of these presumptions are built on false pretences, for instance, a framework of surveillance that is veiled by messages of safeguarding. More pressing still are how this framework is structured and indeed its implication in how the message is delivered. O'Donnell (2017) shares our concerns with the ERG22+, most particularly as it is a doctrine that has not been peer-reviewed and is based on a limited evidential foundation (Knudsen 2018). Instead, the ERG22+ is a toolkit of imagined potential to vulnerability—a pre-criminal framework, where the ultimate emphasis is on identifying the crime before it is committed, which in itself offers potential for misidentification. The doctrine of securitised education follows the influence of Prevent where emphasis on awareness of potential risks, neatly encapsulated in the 'codified' rules of what the risks are, sends a deeper message of how to image dangers in that pre-criminal space. What are those dangers that we should be vigilant towards? The imaginations framed by education deliver how this is understood, contemplated, and visualised by students and teachers and their wider social networks position and strengthen how the message is relayed in the classroom and in broader contexts.

To give an example, consider the act of running into a burning building to rescue someone. This is one example of how we might contemplate what a risk looks like and how we could combat that risk or even help those in danger. We are unlikely to have to run into a burning building as it is a rare occurrence and we would expect trained personnel to perform the task; however, this does not prevent us from thinking about what it may be like to perform such a task. This, of course, may be the ultimate act of someone wishing to prevent deaths in a fire; however, the message does serve to enforce fire safety messages and vigilance to danger that promote subsequent precautionary action such as not leaving a frying pan on high heat unattended because it may cause a house fire with catastrophic results. In a context of securitisation in education, the message of what is vulnerability, what is to be looked for, or how to 'spot' danger informs predispositions towards those who may be potentially at risk or risky and encourage the inner fire-fighter in us to act on clues that for an untrained fire-fighter may be perilous.

But the more pressing issue here is the shaping of the message being told and the focus of this message. Recent statistics do show that the proportion of individuals supported by Channel as a result of far-right cases has risen from a quarter in 2015–2016 to one-third between 2016 and 2017 (Home Office 2018a, b), implying that the public is more aware of different forms of extremism and that the government is doing more to address this issue. However, much of the critical attention paid to Prevent continues to identify that the Muslim population in the UK is the predominant focus of such a strategy, and this continues to compound perceptions of a suspect community. As we have sought to demonstrate, these efforts to challenge and disrupt extremism presume a position of certainty in one's own understanding around identification. However, ambiguity around what to look for, persistent harmful stereotypes, and 'intuitive' but unsubstantiated modes of thought expose the fallacy of this 'certainty' and reveal the ease by which a strategy with an uncontroversial starting point (to prevent violence) can allow harmful forms of structural violence (Galtung 1969) that disproportionately affect particular groups. Tasking non-specialists (e.g. lecturers or teachers) with this role only exacerbates the possibility of such dangers and means that some of the harmful impacts of securitising education and promoting vigilance/suspicion in the classroom such as alienation or the silencing of voices become more likely.

What this new critical literature highlights is the linear and limiting stance that governmental policy has had on responding to the tensions of assimilation, but also in seeking to inhibit the tiny minority of those who commit act of terrorism. Arendt (1961) states that education should not be used for political gain, and yet the Prevent Duty has resulted in educators finding themselves tasked with contributing to counter-terrorism objectives in a manner that frames students as both 'at risk' and 'risky' and threatens to see those very students withdrawing from discussion, becoming more isolated, and having their educational horizons limited through fear of stigmatisation. This securitisation of education limits freedom of thought and expression and puts educators in an uncomfortable position of having to manage their role developing the critical faculties of students alongside a legal requirement to partake in counter-extremism.

## Transparency and Scrutiny

Our aim in writing this book has been to consider a number of pressing questions around the manner in which governmental responses to terrorism, extremism, and radicalisation have been conceptualised and actioned within education. A number of important themes have been identified in this endeavour, but the ambiguity and uncertainty that surround both the strategy and the duty provide recurrent frustrations and beg the question of whether more transparency can be achieved around UK counter-extremism. The evidential foundations of various aspects of the Prevent Duty appear limited as does the ability to gain access to information pertaining to how it is currently operating.

On the latter point, this is not to say that such information does not exist, and we do draw some solace from the recent Home Office (2018a, b) publication which provides an overview of the number reported to the Prevent programme. In this we learn, during 2016/17, 6093 individuals were referred to the programme due to concerns of vulnerability and potential to become involved in terrorism. A total of 1,976 (32%) of the referrals came from the education sector. We also learn the majority of referral were in the London region (25%), that 2199 (36%) of the 6093 referrals required no further action, that 57% of referral were for those under 20 years old, and that 61% of referrals concerned Islamist extremism and 16% right-wing extremism. Of those referred for Islamist extremism, 29% were under 15. Moreover, the number of referrals was down 20% in 2016/17 compared to the previous year. CONTEST (HM Government 2018: 39) lays out the government's plans to publish these sorts of statistical reports every year, and regular information pertaining to Prevent's operation is very welcome; however, what remains pressing for us are answers to the composition of those referred from the educational sector; for example, how many were from the HE sector and of those how many required further action?

In trying to gain some more clarity on issues such as these as well as the impact of Prevent and the CTSA, we submitted a Freedom of Information (FOI) request to the Home Office.[1] We asked for details on the number of referrals made, how these referrals corresponded to the Channel assessment framework, did referrals lead to participation in deradicalisation programmes, and completion rates of university staff on CTSA training programmes. We learnt that 29,238 HE/FE staff (this includes any post-secondary school study towards a degree or a vocational qualification) have received training. Nevertheless, our other requests were declined on the basis of Section 22 and Section 36 of the Freedom of Information Act. In the first instance, Section 22 refers to information that may be printed in the future, but no further detail was supplied, that is, possible date of publication. Section 36 refers to the fact that releasing the information may prejudice the effective conduct of public affairs, and there is a lack of public interest in the disclosure. The response lacked precision, did not adequately answer our questions, and did not help in our endeavours to demystify the operation of the Prevent Duty within education.

What it did reveal was that at the time of the FOI, the number of staff who received training was limited. While 29,238 of all HE/FE staff may have participated in the training, there are 201,380 academic staff and 208,750 non-academic staff working in UK universities alone (Universities

[1] We submitted this FOI on December 1, 2016, and received our reply on January 4, 2017.

UK 2017). The inconsistency of training across the sector will be a contributing factor when lecturers express their lack of knowledge when tasked with identifying radical behaviours, and this lack of knowledge exists while staff are bound by the CTSA mandate to monitor and report. However, this is not to say that more training represents the answer to all the issues raised here. While it may serve to increase lecturers' feelings of being more knowledgeable about the subject and, in turn, their confidence identifying the signs of radicalisation, it does not address deeper issues within the knowledge base that informs the training (Lloyd and Dean 2015)—a significant problem that will be hard to overcome until all the research informing aspects like the ERG22+ are published and debated (see Guardian 2016).

Clearly, with issues related to terrorism there will be legitimate reasons why some information cannot be shared. However, given the new CONTEST strategy's stated desire to provide 'increased transparency and oversight' (HM Government 2018: 8), there is a tremendous opportunity to do just this in relation to the specified authorities defined and mandated by the CTSA and more importantly the evidence base that underpins UK counter-extremism as a whole. The recently established Commission for Countering Extremism announced in 2018 their 'evidence drive' to provide a comprehensive report into what is known around extremism, a drive for which the government immediately committed to sharing information for (Commission for Countering Extremism 2018).

This Commission has not been without its own controversy and criticism (Grierson 2018), but putting this to one side, the evidence drive described here and the government's willingness to share information do not go far enough in reflecting critically on all the factors that contribute to these challenges, in particular, the government's own strategy. Of course, evidence produced in the Commission's research may well go on to influence and redirect governmental strategy, but if the message in CONTEST about a desire to be more transparent around these sensitive issues is a genuine one, then this should go further than just the 'external' issues with the presumption that governmental responses are fundamentally sound. With the expansion of counter-extremism and counter-terrorism in the public sector, the need to scrutinise the evidence base and the underpinning logics that have informed this strategy has never been more pressing, and the failure to do so threatens a counter-productive approach with harmful consequences for those responsibilised and those deemed simultaneously risky and at risk.

## Concluding Remarks

The findings in this book offer some semblance as to how we can begin to understand the effects of the CTSA in education. Universities must be less rigid in the responsibility handed down to them, and furthermore, university staff must make their own decisions as to how they carry out their duty (if at all). The CTSA has been accused of hindering opportunities to engage in open debate, restricting research around 'sensitive' topics and creating a divide between staff and students. This is a counter-productive approach and one reminiscent of the heavy-handed government approaches of the past (see Hillyard 1993). Moreover, lecturers' responsibilities have grown ever wider in terms of administration and pastoral care in addition to their teaching and research. The CTSA adds security expectations upon these day-to-day duties. The argument here is not intended to highlight that lecturers are frequently spread thin across a range of diverse roles but, instead, that these extra statutory duties, a sense of ambiguity around the specifics of these duties, and a questionable evidence base for them could be counter-productive and dangerous.

Notwithstanding the threats posed by terrorism and the uncontroversial desire that the government has to prevent politically motivated violence against civilians, there are clearly concerns about the practical implications of making this a legal requirement to 'inform' on students as potential extremists. In addition, universities face a challenge to maintain their openness, tolerance, and freedom of expression. Through formally enshrining this duty in law and deputising academic staff into a programme of state surveillance, the government risks breeding suspicion between students and staff. The staff we spoke to remain uncomfortable with the CTSA because they are being asked to act in a way that runs contrary to their understanding of what their role as educators is, and rather than concentrating on creating spaces for free expression and critical discussion on potentially challenging subjects, they are having to balance this with a newly mandated security role.

## References

Arendt, H. 1961. *Between Past and Future*. New York: Viking Press.

Ball, S. J. 2012. "Performativity, Commodification and Commitment: An I-Spy Guide to the Neoliberal University", *British Journal of Educational Studies*, 60(1): 17–28.

Ball, K., Canhoto, A., Daniel, E., Dibb, S., Meadows, M. and Spiller, K. 2015. *The Private Security State?: Surveillance, consumer Data and the War on Terror.* Copenhagen: Copenhagen Business School Press.

Beck, U. 2002. "The terrorist threat: World risk society revisited", *Theory, culture & society*, 19(4): 39–55.

Commission for Countering Extremism. 2018. "Press release: Commission for Countering Extremism launches evidence drive", *gov.uk*, available at: https://www.gov.uk/government/news/commission-for-countering-extremism-launches-evidence-drive

Foucault, M. 2007. *Security, territory, population.* London: Palgrave Macmillan.

Fricker, M. 2007. *Epistemic Injustice: Power and the Ethics of Knowing.* Oxford: Oxford University Press.

Gandy, O. H. 2012. *Coming to Terms with Chance: Engaging Rational Discrimination and Cumulative Disadvantage.* London: Ashgate Publishing.

Guardian. 2016. "Anti-Radicalisation Strategy Lacks Evidence Base in Science." Available at: https://www.theguardian.com/politics/2016/sep/29/anti-radicalisation-strategy-lacks-evidence-base-in-science

Grierson, J. 2018. "Choice of new UK anti-extremism chief criticised as 'alarming'", *The Guardian*, available at: https://www.theguardian.com/politics/2018/jan/24/leading-muslim-campaigner-sara-khan-head-anti-extremism-drive

Ford, K. 2017. "Developing a peace perspective on counter-extremist education", *Peace Review*, 29(2): 144–152.

Galtung, J. 1969. "Violence, peace and peace research", *Journal of Peace Research*, 6(3), pp. 167–191.

Hillyard, P. 1993. *Suspect Community: People's Experiences of the Prevention of Terrorism Acts in Britain.* London: Pluto Press.

HM Government. 2018. "Counter-terrorism strategy (CONTEST) 2018". Available at: https://www.gov.uk/government/publications/counter-terrorism-strategy-contest-2018

Home Office. 2018a. "Individuals referred to and supported through the Prevent Programme, April 2016 to March 2017". Available at https://assets.publishing.service.gov.uk/government/uploads/system/uploads/attachment_data/file/694002/individuals-referred-supported-prevent-programme-apr2016-mar2017.pdf

Home Office. 2018b. "Press release: New figures show improved referrals to Prevent and a rise in far-right concerns", *Gov.uk*, available at: https://www.gov.uk/government/news/new-figures-show-improved-referrals-to-prevent-and-a-rise-in-far-right-concerns

Knudsen, R. A. (2018). Measuring radicalisation: risk assessment conceptualisations and practice in England and Wales. *Behavioral Sciences of Terrorism and Political Aggression*, 1–18.

Lloyd, M., and C. Dean. 2015. "The Development of Structured Guidelines for Assessing Risk in Extremist Offenders", *The Journal of Threat Assessment and Management*, 2(1): 40–52.

McGhee, D. 2010. *Security, citizenship and human rights: shared values in uncertain times.* Basingstoke: Palgrave Macmillan.

O'Donnell, A. 2017. "Pedagogical injustice and counter-terrorist education", *Education, citizenship and social justice, 12*(2): 177–193.

O'Donnell, A. 2018. "Contagious ideas: vulnerability, epistemic injustice and counter-terrorism in education", *Educational Philosophy and Theory*, 50(10): 981–997.

Said, E. 1995. *Orientalism.* New York: Pantheon.

Spiller, K., Awan, I. and Whiting, A. 2018. "'What does terrorism look like?': university lecturers' interpretations of their Prevent duties and tackling extremism in UK universities", *Critical Studies on Terrorism*, 11(1): 130–150.

Universities UK. 2017. "Higher Education in numbers". Available at: https://www.universitiesuk.ac.uk/facts-and-stats/Pages/higher-education-data.aspx

# Index[1]



[1] Note: Page numbers followed by 'n' refer to notes.



I. Awan et al., *Terrorism in the Classroom*, Palgrave Studies in Risk, Crime and Society,
https://doi.org/10.1007/978-3-030-01710-1

Printed by Printforce, the Netherlands